RIVEN™

THE SEQUEL TO MYST®

The Official Strategy Guide

Rick Barba

Prima Publishing
Rocklin, California

916-632-4400
www.primagames.com

table of contents

introduction

Well, here we are again.

Welcome to the official, Cyan-endorsed strategy guide for *Riven*. In case you didn't know, *Riven* is the world that *Myst* built. If you're one of the millions who loved *Myst*, I guarantee you'll love *Riven*. And if you're one of the nearly 1 million players who turned to Prima's *Myst: The Official Strategy Guide* for sure guidance, I guarantee you'll find this book equally helpful.

how to use this book

Riven: The Official Strategy Guide features a simple, two-part format. Even if you've never consulted a strategy guide before, you'll find this book extremely easy to use.

Part One, "Riven Journal," continues the Myst Journal so popular in *Myst: The Official Strategy Guide.* The same intrepid Everyman continues his sojourn across the Ages, helping Atrus and battling bewilderment every step of the way. As in the *Myst* guide, his approach is observational, suggesting general strategies that guide you gently toward answers. Read the Riven Journal for hints if you don't necessarily want puzzle solutions right away.

Part Two, "Riven Quick Guide," provides detailed maps and a no-nonsense, step-by-step solution path through *Riven.* Of course, *Riven,* like *Myst,* is not strictly linear in structure. So keep in mind that the Riven Quick Guide offers but one of many ways to complete the game.

foreword

It was the end of summer 1991. Soldiers were leaving the Persian Gulf. The Soviet Union was taking its last gasp. And we had just received the funding for something that we would call *Myst*.

We had it all planned out. The name had been chosen. The story was going to be something about an island. The artwork would be hand-painted. The characters would be hand-animated. There would be no dying. There would be no "save-game" function. And the player would be the protagonist, having to rely on his or her own intuition to work through the story.

Pretty good, huh?

A few months into the project we realized that we had no idea what we were doing. Design, graphics, animations, character development, scripting, editing, sound effects, music, interactivity—it was all a mystery to us.

And this is how the creation of *Myst* became a two-year experiment. Ninety percent of our time was spent figuring out how to do things; the other ten percent was spent doing them. So, by the end of it, we were actually incredibly surprised to encounter such success. Our experiment turned into a so-called "hit," and we started thinking, "Hey, we actually know what we're doing! Let's make the sequel! It'll be easy!"

It wasn't.

Riven ended up being a mammoth undertaking, taking a team of over 20 people almost four years to produce. It has been the most grueling, yet the most thrilling, creative experience of our lives. And now, as we wrap things up, we once again begin to believe we know what we're doing. Strange.

Yet, at the same time, it becomes apparent that we are only scratching the surface of this still very undefined medium.

Rand Miller   Robyn Miller   Richard Vander Wende
CYAN, INC.

Riven: The Myst phenomenon continues

I admit it. When I first saw the beta version of *Myst* in 1993 and started writing the official strategy guide, I didn't see "The *Myst* Phenomenon" coming. Nobody did. Four million units later, *Myst* continues to confound critics and industry sages. And now comes *Riven*, one of the most highly anticipated sequels to an entertainment product since *Return of the Jedi.*

What's the *Myst* secret?

Occasionally, I meet people who hate *Myst.* They puzzle at its monumental success. Many of these doubters, I notice, toil in the computer gaming industry. Hard-core "gamers," software execs, media types—they just don't get the *Myst* thing. It really irks them that two-thirds of *Myst* buyers are nongamers. This antipathy gives me a clue to the game's appeal.

My theory: *Myst* (and now *Riven*) is just too pure. Anybody can play it. Gamers hate that. How can it be entertaining to move serenely through one of the most beautiful worlds you've ever seen—a world with an engaging story, a dark secret, and people who need your help? What a drag. Let's go calculate attack vectors and blow up stuff.

Whatever the case, *Myst* is the first great success story of the digital entertainment age. *Newsweek* calls it "an instant classic ... alone in the playing field." The *New York Times* says, "It's reflective, almost cool aesthetic suggests what is possible: image, sound and narrative woven into a new form of experience." *Wired* agrees, declaring *Myst* "the first interactive artifact to suggest that a new art form might very well be plausible."

And now *Riven* writes the next chapter of that story.

MYST

My Myst Journal is now complete.

Here begins Riven.

After taking one last nostalgic tour around the uninhabited Ages linked to Myst, I returned to D'ni (misspelled "Dunny" in my Myst Journal) to find Atrus still scribbling away. He looked up with obvious relief and said, "Thank God you've returned. I need your help."

Apparently, zapping me home wasn't an optio I stepped forward. I remember his last words: " am fighting a foe much greater than my sons could even imagine." He handed over his journal, warning me to keep it well hidden. He can't send me to Riven with a way out, but gave me what appears to be a linking book back to D'ni. It is, in fact, a one-man prison. A trap. I need it to capture Gehn.

Who's Gehn?

I didn't ask.

Atrus had no time to explain. But once I arrived here in Riven, I glanced at his journal. Atrus, I knew, was lured into D'ni exile by his own greedy offspring. Who could be a greater foe than a man's own sons?

Of course: His father.

Wow. Greek tragedy had better family values. The man who taught Atrus the art of the linking books is an evil megalomaniac. Worse, he is a bad writer. Atrus spoke of "the familiar pattern of decay that is the hallmark of my father's work." Apparently, Gehn's Fifth Age is breaking apart. Known as Riven, that Age is also where Catherine is imprisoned. From D'ni, Atrus furiously debugs his father's flawed Riven code, trying to save both his wife and her dying home world. But his "patches" can only delay the inevitable catastrophe.

I slipped the journal into my camera case. Atrus held out the linking book to Riven. Its Gateway Image was blurred, unlike the crisp images in his Myst books. I snapped a photo. Then I hesitated. But the weary concern in Atrus's eyes spurred me to reach out.

I placed my hand upon the page.

temple island

And now I sit on yet another island.

Unlike Myst, this one is inhabited. A blessing? The jury's still out.

Let me bring you up to date:

The Link was painless, as usual. But my arrival wasn't unexpected. Despite his flaws as a linking book author, Gehn knows his interdimensional rip locations: I materialized in a cage. And my arrival alerted a wild-looking guy in a helmet and white coat—a sentry or guard, no doubt. Speaking in a strange tongue, he wrenched the Prison Book from me.

Don't understand Rivenese yet. I think he said something about playing bass for Aerosmith.

Moments later, the guard slapped at his neck—and fell, unconscious. A black-clad figure dragged him away and picked up the Prison Book. To my surprise, this new fellow pulled the lever to open my cage and smashed the lever mechanism with an ax, jamming the bars open permanently. Then like a phantom, he disappeared. I stepped out and looked around.

The island is spectacular.

Like Myst, it bristles with odd structures and mechanisms. Walkways span the cliffs above. A system of rails or cables runs to other islands. I glance over the nearby cliff: My ex-guard lies on a ledge below, a dagger beside him. I turn back to the cell where I arrived. Next to it, an object juts from the ground— a giant version of the same dagger.

Interesting.

Bright lights, big dagger.

telescope

Nearby hulks what seems to be a huge viewing device—an eyepiece, two movable levers, a button. The lens points down at a closed hatch with five buttons. The device seems to lack power, and I can't find an on–off switch.

Nothing works. What is it? Where's the power source?

As I stare at the telescope and jot these notes, a thought strikes me. Atrus asked me to signal him once I've found Catherine.

How?

Time to continue reading the journal of Atrus. Perhaps I'll find the answer there.

journal of atrus

Unsettling. The more I read, the worse it gets. Gehn, destroyer of worlds, is marooned here in Riven. More chilling are these words: "The complexity of the problem is overwhelming."

Riven is dying.

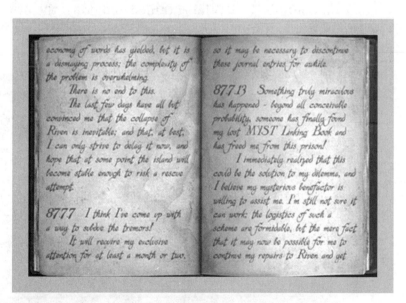

One other note: Atrus duly acknowledges my Myst rescue. My arrival in D'ni with the missing white page of his Myst linking book is dated 87.7.13. What this means, I have no idea. But the next entry—87.7.16—clarifies Atrus's current motives. He gave me no return linking book because he so terribly fears Gehn's escape.

As for the signal I am to give—the Riven Gateway Image is trashed. Atrus can't see or hear me. He can observe only what he calls "basic changes in the Age." So his only suggestion is to investigate an anomaly that appears as a rift somewhere—the "Star Fissure," he calls it. All I have to do is find this rift, exploit its weakness to effect a fundamental change in the Riven Age, and then wait patiently for Atrus while all hell breaks loose.

Sounds easy. I've always enjoyed exploiting anomalous fissures.

Time to explore.

The only egress from the telescope area lay up a stone stairway. At the top, a small opening had been hewn into the rock face. From there, a footbridge extended over a chasm to another opening in the far rocks. The path continued past the entrance and down the other side. I moved across the footbridge for an overview of the island. When I looked back, here's what I saw:

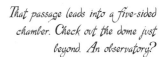
That passage leads into a five-sided chamber. Check out the dome just beyond. An observatory?

The Gate Room

I returned and entered the passage. Inside, a button juts from the wall just outside a fabulous five-sided room, where I sit now, writing. What is this place? A planetarium? A holy place?

What happens if I push the button?

Five sides, two doors. But that far gate is locked. Is there another way through?

Everything is fives—five-pointed stars, five walls, five pillars. Mounted on each pillar is a scarab-like beetle with an eyepiece depicting strange religious icons like stained-glass windows in a church. Four scenes feature the same prominent, god-like figure. My guess—Gehn.

Is this Gehn? If so, he has a serious god complex.

A gate on the rear-left wall is locked. Beyond the gate, a footbridge runs across a chasm to the massive dome structure of brilliant, burnished gold. I couldn't find a lock mechanism, though. So I stepped back outside and pushed the wall button, hoping it would unlock the gate.

The entire room began to rotate!

I watched in awe as the inner chamber made one-fifth of a turn, bringing back memories of the tower rotation code on Myst Island. But now my entry was blocked. Two more turns would bring the far doorway around to my position. I pushed the button two more times and reentered the Gate Room. The doorway I originally entered through had rotated to the rear-right wall. And there—another locked gate. Beyond that, a closed door.

Now what?

side gate entry

Aha! This must be the answer.

I exited the Gate Room and followed a path down to a primitive wooden gate. It was locked, but easy enough to crawl under. I followed a cave passage to a peephole into the Gate Room. Obviously, this was a side passage. I needed only rotate the inner chamber so one of the doorways was on this wall of the room.

This old cave leads to the Gate Room.

Later:

Success! I got in the side door. And across the Gate Room, the other doorway led into a short cave with some kind of pipe and valve. I flipped the valve and listened to steam hiss down the pipe. Where to? The diagram etched on the pipe gave me a pretty good idea.

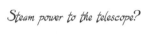

Steam power to the telescope?

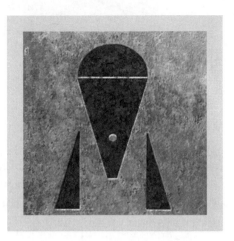

When I climbed back up the passage, I found a power switch just outside the door. I applied what I now call the Myst Rule: Flip any switch that will move. Something happens in the Gate Room. My guess—a gate opened.

More room rotation confirmed my guess—the far-right gate was open, but the door beyond remained closed and locked. I found another power switch, however. This one opened the other locked gate. More rotations brought me back across into the main antechamber, where I rotated the room again to its original setting.

And I was off to the Golden Dome.

Gate Room

to Golden Dome

gate 1

gate 2

handle (opens Gate 1)

handle (opens Gate 2)

Steam Valve

Rotation buttons Gate handles

To Temple

The Golden Dome

I've got a new theory about this dome.

It's not an observatory—no sign of a telescope, anyway. But everything I've seen so far points to a system of steam power. I think the Golden Dome is some sort of central power source for Riven's island cluster. Inside, a huge boiler-like mechanism sprouts five pipes running in five directions. I feel moist heat, and I hear bubbling liquid. Outside, I see the pipes drop into the sea and then rise ashore at other islands.

To what, specifically, do they connect?

Right now, I stand before a plaque on the railing. No doubt it diagrams the power dispersal. But there's some sort of grid code:

Pipes run from Golden Dome to five locations. What do these five grid patterns represent?

A catwalk circles the dome's interior. There's an upper-level catwalk, but I can't reach it from here. For now, I'll follow the lower catwalk.

Drawbridge controls

My steam-power hypothesis held water, if you'll pardon the feeble pun. The lower catwalk exited the far side of the Golden Dome, emerging just beneath a lengthy footbridge. The footbridge ran from the dome's upper catwalk to an island shimmering on the water about a half-mile away. There was no obvious way up to the footbridge, though.

I continued along a walkway to a pipe venting steam into the air.

This valve sends power up to that drawbridge. How do I get up there to lower the darn thing?

I turned the valve handle to cap the vent. This sent steam flowing out a side pipe. I looked up. The side pipe ran directly to a raised drawbridge at the Golden Dome end of the long, interisland footbridge. No movement, though. Powering up certain devices in Riven must be a two-step process: First, you direct steam power to the mechanism. Then you must throw a switch or lever on the device to activate it.

At the end of the walkway, I flipped another pipe valve to send steam power up to the footbridge I crossed earlier, the one connecting the Gate Room to the Golden Dome. The diagram etched on the pipe indicates that footbridge is a drawbridge, too.

This was as far as I could go on the walkway, so I returned through the Golden Dome. Before crossing the bridge to the Gate Room, I gave the lever by the dome entry a yank. Sure enough, the footbridge raised—unfortunately, on my side (the Golden Dome side). I lowered it to continue back through the Gate Room.

OK, it's up. Now what? Can't go anywhere from this side.

Now I sit at the cave passage across the chasm from the Gate Room, writing this update. Actually, I'm stalling. It's pretty dark down there. I don't like dark. It's a vitamin D thing. OK, maybe a bat thing, too. Bats hang out in dark caves, just waiting to shriek in your ear. I know this for a fact.

The Throne Room

The technology of these Ages continues to amaze me.

I found a room carved from the rock halfway down the cave passage. In it, a caged chair sits alone—lurks, really. It has a malevolent aura, this chair. When I approached, its cage bars lifted like the legs of a mechanical spider.

Lighting seemed important here; spotlights encircled the throne, casting brilliant light on whoever might sit there.

Anybody sitting here will glow with serious candlepower.

I chose to sit and update this journal. But first I examined the two viewscreens on the walls. The left screen displays stairs leading up to a platform. Above the platform hang cables like those I've seen stretching from island to island. Some sort of terminal, perhaps?

The other screen displays a room lined with pillars. I flipped a switch next to the screen. In the display, a door opened. It seemed to lead outside.

Where is it?

This switch opens the door the viewer shows. Where?

As I sit here in the chair I notice a button. When I push it, the cage lowers. A microphone-like device drops before me. I pull a switch and hear a hum: Something's powering up; I'm not sure what. In any case, whoever sits in this chair maintains surveillance via these monitors. But surveillance of what?

Time to continue down the cave passage.

Gehn's Temple

Now I understand.

The passage leads to the pillar-lined room I'd seen in the throne room viewscreen. It is a place of worship. Backlit by yet another five-pointed star, a cage (suspiciously like the one over the throne upstairs) sits between wood carvings of two scaly creatures. They resemble humpbacked whales with tusks. Most unpleasant. Before each idol lay offerings of fruit and flowers.

And I thought Oz was bad.

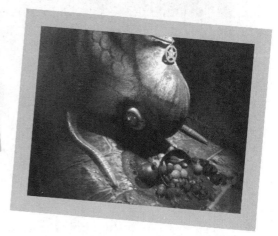

If I meet one of these, I quit.

It isn't hard to guess the scheme here.

Someone sits on the throne upstairs. This person's image and voice project to this temple chamber (filled with cowering Rivenese, no doubt). In my Myst adventures, I encountered a similar device—Achenar's hologram projector in Channelwood. Like grandfather, like grandson, I guess. Does Gehn need this sort of thing to keep the inhabitants of his Age in line?

Or is he just in it for the fruit?

Tram station

The open door leads outside Gehn's temple to yet another remarkably cool Riven device. At the bottom of a platform is a small podium with a glowing blue button on top. I pushed the button and noticed movement in the distance. Something emerged from the tall, heavily wooded island across the way. I looked closer. A pod-like metal car zipped along the cables over the water.

Had I called a cab?

I grew excited. A way to escape Temple Island! But as the car approached, I began to wonder just who might be aboard.

Guys in white coats?

Villagers bearing fruit?

Gehn himself?

I've always been a big fan of public transportation.

The car arrived, thankfully empty. I climbed aboard. Turned out to be a self-service tram. Fortunately, the controls were designed for idiots like me. After a few weeks I got the car rotated and ready to go. Then I decided to jot this journal update before I try flipping the power switch.

I want to document any fatal mistakes. Hey, that's just the kind of adventurer I am.

jungle island

Interesting trip. I'd tell you more, but I need to go find my stomach now. I'm pretty sure I dropped it somewhere near the tram's third curve. Did I tell you I hate roller coasters? Perhaps I should have. Then this craven fear might be less surprising.

Well, I survived, anyway.

tram station: jungle island

After the spasms subsided, I stepped from the tram car. Heading for the stairs in a nearby cave passage, I glimpsed something odd—a big wooden eye in the rock wall. When I touched it, the eye rotated. An odd symbol is etched on the back.

And the eye makes odd noises. It … chirps?

Chirping eye, symbol on back.

But wait. It gets weirder. I tried to extract the eye. Nothing doing. So I turned away, entered the cave passage, and climbed the stairs. Halfway up, I turned to get a last look at the eye.

Here's what I saw:

Very amphibious, if you ask me.

That's a frog if ever I saw one.

Note the location of the wooden eye in the shape of the cave opening. That's no coincidence. Surely it means something.

Anyway, I climbed the stairs and sat down to write this. Another blue tram call button is installed here. Outside, stone stairs lead up and down. Which way? I think I'll start low.

sunner rock

Wildlife!

Descending the steep stairway, I came upon quite a sight. Two incredible animals lazed on rocks in a gorgeous, aquamarine lagoon. One raised its head. I froze—which was good, because, as I discovered later, they spook easily. I inched forward, moving only when their heads were lowered.

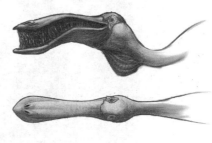

"Sunners"

These sunners (as I'll call them) look like seals with long necks and huge snouts. The snout is remarkable. I'm no marine biologist, but their jaws appear lined with baleen (thin, bony plates that strain food from the water, like some whales have). When I stepped onto the beach, one of the sunners raised its head again and barked. Quite a sound. When I turned to stroll down the beach, both slipped into the water and disappeared.

I rounded the lagoon. It was beautiful. The water, crystal clear. Too bad restless tectonic plates are ripping the place apart. At the end of the beach, I sat to write and look for more sunners. But then I saw something lodged in the rocks out in the lagoon.

Another wooden eye!

Same as the idols in Gehn's temple!

Remembering the frog outline of the cave opening, I squinted at the rock formation. After a moment, I saw it—the same whale-like, hump-backed creature I saw back in Gehn's temple. I waded across a sandbar to the eye and rotated it. The sound was indeed cetaceous, but with a chilling edge. And I found another symbol etched on the back side. Animal sounds and shapes, paired with odd symbols.

What's the correlation?

village lake overview

Weird physics reigns in Riven.

From the lagoon, I returned to the path and followed it through a long, twisting tunnel. Fortunately, tiny globe lanterns lit the way. As I emerged onto a catwalk, a native sentry sounded an alarm and signaled below. I crept forward, expecting a volley of arrows. But the sentry disappeared. I could see no signs of life.

And then I saw the lake.

Are those water holes down there?

At first glance, it was just that—a lake. Surrounded by the high cliff walls of an ancient, crumbling crater, it was as translucent and beautiful as the sunners' lagoon. But then I looked closer.

The lake had "holes."

Holes in the water!

I scrambled down ladders to the lake surface. A path led to a ladder that dropped down into a quivering water hole. Incredible! At the bottom, I noticed the twin rails of a track.

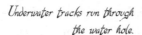

Underwater tracks run through the water hole.

An underwater track circuit rings the lake from hole to hole. Looks like another tram system; the holes must be tram stops. Stunning. I sit on the platform above the tracks, writing these journal notes and fighting the urge to thrust my arm through the shimmering, vertical water wall.

Bug-Eye Basin

After a rest, I climbed back up to a small rock plateau. As I nearly passed the crude earthen basin, yet another wooden eye caught my attention. Embedded in the basin, this eye makes a rubbing, clicking sound when rotated. Remembering the other eyes, I viewed it from different perspectives, looking for the distinctive outline of another creature. But nothing looked familiar.

Another eye, another symbol.

Thirsty, I gave the basin spigot a twist. Water bubbled up around the wooden eye, then stopped abruptly. I tried the spigot again. Nothing. I looked at the water. An image began to coalesce in a strange, Rorschach sort of way. Call me nutty, but it looks like a bug.

Here, take a peek:

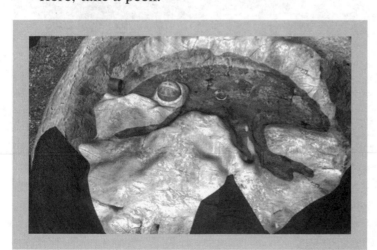

That's a bug, right?

From the basin plateau, I saw a number of interesting structures on the cliffs surrounding the lake. I climbed back up to the path and retraced my route all the way back past the sunners' lagoon. From there, I headed back up the stone steps.

The Jungle Gate

The path led over a suspension bridge to a clear-cut area. Great tree stumps covered the hillside. I remembered the odd religious icons depicted back in the Temple Island Gate Room. In one, trees were felled to make sacred books. Linking books, perhaps? If Gehn is trapped here, he's surely seeking a way out.

Spotted owls, look out. Here comes Gehn.

Up ahead I saw a gate, and behind it, a dense forest. Before entering, I veered off a side path and found a small cart on an underground track. Given the setting, I assume it's a logging car, used to transport felled timber to some other location, perhaps another island.

Where does this logging car go?

    I turned and approached the gate. There, a chance encounter confirmed an earlier observation. A large beetle was crawling up the gate post. As I snapped a quick photo, it spread its wings to fly. I recognized the wingspread! It was the golden scarab on the pillars in the Gate Room.

    As it flew away, the bug buzzed.

    Yes! The same "rubbing" sound emitted by the wooden eye in the water basin. So the shape formed by the basin water was a bug, after all.

That voice, those wings ... I know that bug!

So far, then: Three wooden eyes clearly match up with three Riven Age creatures. Given the preoccupation with "fives" around here, my guess is that two more wooden eyes exist somewhere. Of course, I still have no clue what it all means. My mission is to find Gehn and trap him. But maybe on Riven, all eyes look to Gehn.

giant dagger

This forest is spectacular! The trees are massive old-growth beauties, and a phosphorescent blue fungus grows wild in the deep shade. The path runs directly under a rumbling, rotating dome. Nearby juts another giant dagger, where rough-hewn steps descend into a hole in the forest floor. And there—another wooden eye.

The symbol's a mystery, but I'd know that bark anywhere.

I could find no animal silhouette. But when I rotated the eye, the sound was unmistakable—a sunner bark. Eye number four clearly matches the lagoon creature.

After my discovery, I returned to the path, happy in the knowledge that I'm cleverly piecing together clues for no apparent purpose.

Tusk-whale idol (elevator)

Under the rumbling, spinning dome I hit a fork in the path. Being right-handed, I went right, down a lane to yet another carved likeness of the humpbacked tusk-whale. The creature is clearly a powerful cultural icon in Riven.

An upper walkway ran to the top of this particular idol. I found a power switch atop a nearby post. The idol's mouth dropped open—an eerie, tooth-lined staircase.

Into the belly of the beast.

● Inside, I found a tram call button and an elevator. A quick trip down revealed the tram station. But I wasn't ready to leave this island yet. So I rode to the top, where a sturdy metal catwalk wound through the treetops. Shades of Channelwood!

Rotating Dome/Kinetoscope

The dome lay just ahead. At a fork in the catwalk, I went left and examined the spinning structure. A sequence of circular symbols ringed the dome. One, I noted, was highlighted yellow. The other fork of the catwalk ended at a small device that looked like a viewfinder. I looked in the eyepiece.

A kinetoscope!

The shuttered viewer focused on the rotating dome symbols, creating an illusion of motion. A button atop the scope did nothing, it seemed—until I hit it precisely when the yellow symbol appeared.

To open dome, hit button when yellow symbol appears.

The dome stopped spinning and slid open.

What now? I hurried to the dome. Through a glass window in the open slot I could see a book. Under the window—a scale with five sliders and a button. Looks like I need a five-number code. What sort of book would be in such a well-protected place?

I had a pretty good idea.

But if it's a linking book, where does it link to?

The watchtower

OK, I'm sitting on another throne—a throne with a view. Truly, one could feel like a god up here. I can see everything.

How I got here:

From the dome, I continued up the path to a small tower on a cliff overlooking the lake. Inside the tower, a chair nestled snugly in the bleached jawbone of a tusk-whale. So these aquatic creatures aren't mythical. Guess I won't be doing any bodysurfing.

I sat and pushed a lever. The chair began to rotate and rise.

Gehn's watchtower?

What a view!

I can see a cluster of spherical huts on the far cliff. Directly below is a strange cone-shaped cage. Its base platform was open at first, but I pushed the chair's right-hand lever and it slid shut. A narrow plank connects a smaller platform at the top of the cage to a catwalk running along the nearby cliff wall. What is this thing? It looks ceremonial.

Right lever operates base of platform below.

I must reach that village somehow. Perhaps the natives can lead me to Gehn.

The village

I'm an object of fear. Hilarious as that seems, it's got me stymied. People are running from me. No one will talk.

To get here, I retraced my route to the tusk-whale elevator and rode down. As I moved through the forest, I encountered a small girl. She ran, but I managed to snap a photo.

Under the dome, I tried the other fork, veering right. Stairs spanned a thundering volcanic fissure. I wondered if this might be the Star Fissure, the "rift" I'm supposed to "exploit." But it didn't make sense—a crevasse of molten lava? I continued up through another wooden gate, then followed the path down a blue-lit, eerie cave passage.

Halfway down, I came upon a primitive cave painting. Its implications were unsettling:

Almighty Riven god feeds folks to the fish?

My approach triggered a flurry of activity in the village. People ran, gathered up children, and so on. By the time I got there, every hut was sealed. Not a soul out. I climbed to a rock ledge. It held a kiln and several ceremonial urns. More interesting, however, was the wheeled iron sphere. Clearly, it rides those underwater rails on the lake bed.

Lower sub to the underwater tracks. Note: Access dock is back under the bug basin. Backtrack!

I gave the nearby handle a yank. A hoist lowered the sub into the water hole below. Looking down, I recognized the access dock. It was the hole just past the bug-eye basin, where I'd been earlier.

submarine circuit

Ahoy!

OK, so maybe I'm not exactly 20,000 leagues under the sea. But how many people can say they've captained a submarine?

It was a long trek back around the island, but I found a bit of a shortcut: After following the catwalks back to the wooden gate, I continued *past* it. Stairs led directly up to the clear-cut area of the forest. From there it was easy to work my way back past the lagoon and the bug basin to the dock ladder. I climbed into the submarine and experimented with the controls.

Here's what I learned:

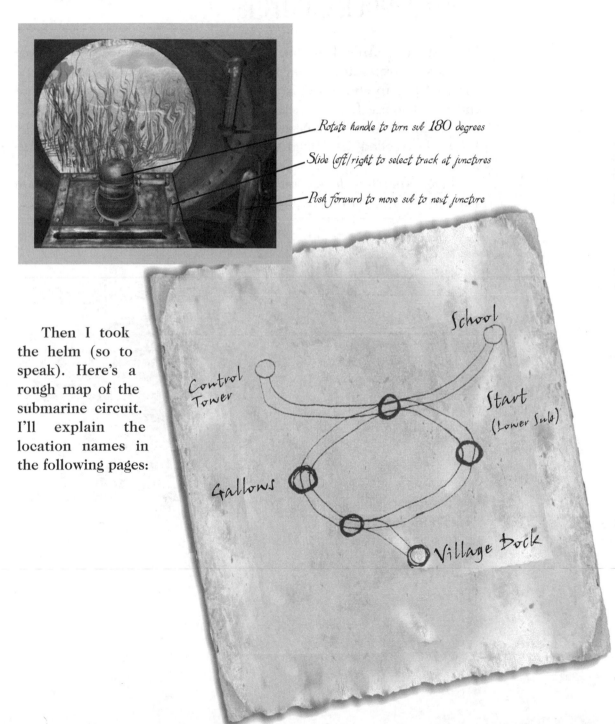

Rotate handle to turn sub 180 degrees

Slide left/right to select track at junctures

Push forward to move sub to next juncture

Then I took the helm (so to speak). Here's a rough map of the submarine circuit. I'll explain the location names in the following pages:

School

Control Tower

Start (Lower Sub)

Gallows

Village Dock

tower: pock controls

My first turns around the lake were fun but frustrating. Because the ramps were retracted, I could exit the sub at only one other dock. There, I had to climb iron rungs up a sheer cliff face into a tower at the top. I found five levers set in the wall—two up, three down. I pushed up the middle lever and turned to a view slot overlooking the lake: I'd extended the dock access ramp of the cone-shaped cage platform.

Five levers, five docks, five access ramps. Realizing the up position *extends* the ramps, I flipped up all five levers.

Push all levers up to extend all dock access ramps over the lake's submarine terminals.

Then it was back to *Das Boot* for further undersea adventures.

school room

The more I learn of Gehn, the creepier he seems.

My next stop on the sub circuit was a small hut—a school, clearly. Benches in rows fill the single room inside. Strange writing covered the crude chalkboards on the front wall. An "alphabet" lines the side walls. A globe-like cage with a crank handle turns out to be a hologram projector.

Could this be Gehn?

I gave the handle a turn. A talking head appeared and intoned a formal greeting. The only word I recognized was "D'ni." The head resembled the figures in the Gate Room religious icons, and I knew: This was Gehn.

OK, that was bad enough.

But then I found a gruesome Rivenese counting game. Two stick figures hang upside-down from what are clearly a pair of gallows. At the base is an open-mouthed tusk-whale. To play, you rotate the deadly jaws under one victim, then the other. Each rotation displays a random symbol on the front of the base. When the symbol appears, the current victim lowers a few notches toward the tusk-whale.

Is this any way to teach your children numbers?

It seems obvious that each symbol represents a number. And they look familiar. Yes, the symbols on the backs of the wooden eyes!

Later:

Having read in Atrus's journal of Gehn's "myopic mission to restore D'ni civilization," my guess is that these are D'ni numbers. Of course, a device like this teaches children numbers and a whole lot more.

After playing *Fish Feed: The Game* for a while, I managed to decipher the following:

1   2   3   4   5   6   7   8   9   10

The first 10 D'ni numbers.

My guess is this: The numbers on the backs of the wooden eyes create an order—bug is 2, frog is 3, sunner is 4, and the tusk-whale is 5. The numerical order arranges the creatures from smallest to biggest. But I haven't yet found the wooden eye that correlates to 1, the first in the series.

And even if I do, what will it tell me?

Amazing. I've learned so much. And yet I know so little.

gallows

And now I sit atop the tall, cone-shaped cage structure, the final destination in my submarine circuit. What I found here turns my stomach, and adds a note of urgency and caution to my search for Gehn.

The skull motif really adds a cheery touch.

Emerging from the sub, I stepped to the cage platform. Suddenly, I heard a chilling wail. It was the sound I'd heard when rotating the wooden eye on the tusk-whale rock formation in the lagoon. Only this was real, and loud, and nearby.

I stepped away from the water.

I noticed a small handle hanging from a cable. When I gave it a yank, a metal bar dropped from the upper platform. I quickly straddled the bar and rode it to the top. As I hopped off, I noticed a pair of adjustable clamps on either end of the bar. An image of the schoolroom "Hangman" game flashed in my mind.

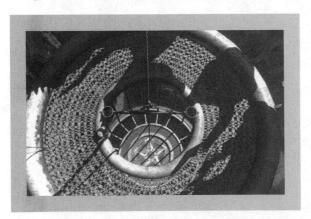

And then its purpose—the purpose of this entire structure—hit me full force.

These clamps are leg-irons.

This is a gallows.

I tried to imagine it: Legs clamped tight. Dangling upside-down. Below, the platform opens. The water roils furiously.

And down you go.

I shook the image from my head and hurried across a plank to the catwalk. There, a cell in the cliff-side housed a prisoner. Did he know his fate? Of course he did. Clearly, Gehn has chosen to make this form of punishment a grisly public spectacle.

Just down the catwalk I found a control wheel. A few quick turns opened the cell. But the prisoner didn't emerge. Was his spirit broken? I went to the cell. He was gone.

Turn wheel, open cell. But where's the prisoner?

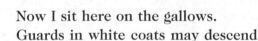

Now I sit here on the gallows.

Guards in white coats may descend at any moment. I'll end up whale food.

But thus far, not a soul in sight, anywhere.

Next step: Scour the holding cell for clues to the prisoner's disappearance.

Holding cell/secret passage

Gehn's enemies are well-organized. I found a remarkable secret exit from the cell. Wasn't hard to find, actually. Not many places to look in a bare cell. I gave the ring mechanism a pull and watched, amazed, as a section of the back wall pulled away. When I stepped through, the passage closed behind me.

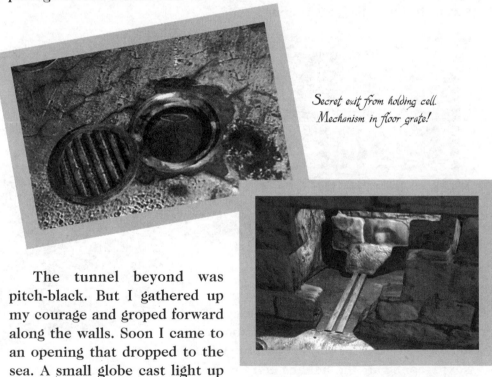

Secret exit from holding cell.
Mechanism in floor grate!

The tunnel beyond was pitch-black. But I gathered up my courage and groped forward along the walls. Soon I came to an opening that dropped to the sea. A small globe cast light up the tunnel. I turned back and groped for more such globes. Working my way from globe to globe, I reached a door carved in the cave wall.

This door swings between two passages.

I pulled the handle. The door swung across the tunnel, revealing a new passage.

stone pillar room

So it comes to this.

A guy sits in a cavernous room, playing with pillars.

Here's where I ended up:

That's a lot of pillars. Some of the etchings look familiar. This bug, for example.

Twenty-five pillars, each etched with a creature icon, are arrayed in a circle around this cavern. Some of the creatures look familiar—sunner, frog, tusk-whale, bug. When I push an icon, that pillar lowers. I suppose there must be a code. But what is it? What does it activate?

Time to get off this island.

Maybe a new setting will freshen my thinking.

Logging car track

Of course, island-hopping can be a white-knuckle experience. Recalling the tram ride from Temple Island, I opted to take the logging car. Surely a cart carrying lumber would move at a nice, leisurely pace.

So I worked my way back up the secret tunnel. Outside the holding cell, I turned right and followed the catwalk to a ladder I extended to the lower catwalk. From there, I worked my way back to the clear-cut area.

Now here I sit in a lumber cart, bringing this journal up to date.

Lumber from this island probably goes to wherever Gehn makes paper—and, hence, his books. I may find him at the other end of this track. In any case, I'm ready to pull the lever and trundle slowly to wherever I end up.

book assembly island

Whoever designed Riven's interisland transportation systems needs a better grasp of g-force. Halfway through the water-tube ride on the logging car, I felt my cheeks pulling away from my gums. I saw quantum physics. It's not just a theory, man.

Then I got dumped into a wood chipper.

Boy, I'm glad it was turned off. These things weren't made for people, you know. Soft tissue really gums up the gears.

crater Lake

Anyway, this chipper sits on the bank of an ancient crater lake. The water's turquoise opacity suggests great depths. Several other structures squat nearby; this is Riven's publishing center. Logs roll in, get churned into piles of sawdust, boiled into pulp, and pressed into pages. I recognize the machines of the process as depicted in the Gate Room icon.

Elements of paper manufacture-wood chipper, boiler-just like the Gate Room icon scene.

I also see a balcony high on the cliff-side with a pair of doors. Beyond that, a catwalk runs along the precipice. But I can spot only two ways up the cliff—a long ladder under the balcony, and a massive boiler pipe that curls up the cliff like giant snake. Unfortunately, the ladder ends at a locked hatch on the balcony's underside. So I'll focus my attention on the boiler.

Only two ways up cliff-ladder, pipe.

valve controls

The boiler controls, of course, didn't work.

But I'm learning the ways of Riven. Remembering the power technology I'd seen on Temple Island, I looked for a steam pipe. Sure enough, I found one running out to a central valve in the middle of the lake. The valve regulates power to three locations—the boiler, the wood chipper, and some unseen device in the nearby cliff.

I turned the valve to the boiler setting.

Middle valve setting powers boiler controls.

wood chip Boiler

This thing is no tea kettle. It's a massive tank with a solid brick housing. After much experimentation, I learned how to get inside the boiler pipe. It's a three-part process—turn off the furnace, drain the tank, raise the floor grate. This last step requires a simple reroute of steam power using the valve switch just left of the boiler controls.

Use these controls to turn off the heat, drain the water, and raise the boiler grate.

Once inside the pipe, I found the going slow and dark. I finally emerged and dropped to a worn path overlooking the ocean. As I climbed the path, I could just glimpse the roof of a spectacular building nestled behind the jagged cliff-top to the right.

The path ended at the high balcony I'd seen from the beach. There, on the balcony's floor, was the hatch that blocked access from the ladder below. I unlatched it. Now I have a quick route down to the lake.

I turned to face the double doors off the balcony. And I wondered: Would these lead me to Gehn?

This hatch leads down a ladder to the beach.

frog Trap

The answer: No. But they did lead me to frogs.

That's right. Frogs. A twisting metal walkway beyond the doors led to an odd contraption under a humming ventilation fan. The device was simple enough to operate once I got it powered up. (This required a trip back the steam pipe valve in the middle of the lake.)

Every great man needs a frog catcher.

At first, I admit, I was stumped. I opened the top and put a food pellet in the center disk. Then I pulled a handle to lower the device into unseen depths. Nothing happened. *What the hell is this thing?* I examined the fan, wondering what it might be ventilating. I sat down, took a rest. Suddenly I heard a snap far below. I yanked the handle to pull up the trap. I opened it to see a reddish frog. It chirped and hopped away.

It was the same chirp I'd heard when I rotated the first wooden eye near the frog-shaped cave.

footbridge to temple island

Gehn's a tricky one.

I spent much fruitless time looking for a route from the balcony/frog-trap area to the cliff catwalk that leads to the hidden building. In and out of the balcony, in and out, in and out. Nothing. Finally, in disgust, I slammed shut the balcony entry doors from the inside. And there was the answer.

Concealed behind the open double doors had been a pair of passages, one on either side. Closing the doors revealed these secret entries.

Close double doors to find secret passages!

The one to the right led directly to the hidden building. On the way I found a lever, which I pulled, of course. (My personal motto: *Be intrusive!*) I heard a mechanism deactivate. What? Noting the power cable running from the lever in two directions—back to the balcony, and forward to the hidden building—I moved on. The hidden building was locked, so I continued forward through a short tunnel.

When I emerged, here's what I saw:

This leads to that drawbridge I powered up on Temple Island a couple of years ago.

I trudged on across the bridge. At the far end, I came to the drawbridge I'd seen from below on Temple Island. I lowered it and entered the Golden Dome.

golden dome: bridging the catwalk gaps

I followed the catwalk around the curve to the end. There, I turned a wheel to extend the retracted section of the catwalk. Easy enough.

As I crossed the newly extended catwalk, I glanced left out a side door. A section of the walk was missing. But I continued down the stairs, out past the steam pipe that powered the drawbridge, and on to the tunnel entrance. There, I noticed a power button on the wall. I pushed it. Nothing happened.

I looked up to see the catwalk with a missing section above me:

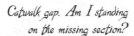

Catwalk gap. Am I standing on the missing section?

Then I looked down.

Aha! A section of walkway at my feet connected to a pair of grooves running up the side of the wall—right to the gap in the upper catwalk! But how do I raise this section?

I hustled upstairs to the gap.

Here's the gap again.

I looked down. Then I turned back to the dome. There, next to the doorway, was a button. I pushed it, and the missing section ascended into place, bridging the gap.

Since I was up there, anyway, I crossed the new section and followed the catwalk, which passed over another rotating dome. It led to a door that opened with a simple pull of a switch. I entered and found myself just outside the Gate Room.

This outer door leads into the Gate Room.

I recognized the place. This was the locked door outside the rightmost of the two gated passages from the Gate Room. Now it was open.

Rotating Dome (Temple Island)

This seems like an awful lot of busy work. It better pay off. Or I'll file complaints.

I went all the way back down to lower catwalk, past the steam pipe again, to the button on the wall. Because the missing section of catwalk was now raised, the button was active. I pushed it; a hydraulic lift lowered me to a tunnel below. I followed this out to a stairway that climbed to the rotating dome.

I used the kinetoscope as before.

Here's the symbol that opens the
Temple Island dome.

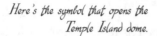

As the dome opened, I noticed
one of the large power pipes from
the Golden Dome fed directly into it.
My guess: The other four pipes lead to rotating domes
on the other islands. Again, the Golden Dome seems to be a central
power source for these rotating domes.

I decided to head back to Book Assembly Island (as I'm calling it,
for obvious reasons). But I made one quick detour on the way. As I
rounded the catwalk inside the Golden Dome, I stopped to raise the
bridge to the Gate Room.

This time I'll leave it up.

This clearly connects the Gate Room to a higher level in the Golden Dome. Maybe I can find another way into the Gate Room so I can access whatever lies above.

Rotating Dome (Book Assembly Island)

I found another rotating dome. But this time, I see no way to stop the spinning. Where's the kinetoscope? Wait, I'm getting ahead of myself.

Let me bring you up to date:

From the Golden Dome, I trekked back across the long interisland footbridge, past the hidden building—which I'm convinced holds answers—and back to the spot just inside the double doors of the balcony. I'd almost forgotten that another passage runs down the opposite side. I followed it to another rotating dome.

But this one had no kinetoscope! How could I stop the rotation?

First I looked up. This dome sits in a cavern. The power pipe from the Golden Dome curls in through a round hole blasted in the ceiling.

Book Assembly rotating dome is underground! Only this crater hole in the ceiling would give away its location from above.

Then I walked around the dome, trying to determine the high-lighted symbol. These circular symbols, one associated with each dome so far, must signify something.

Then I caught sight of a lens embedded in the rock wall.

Could that be the kinetoscope viewfinder? If so, how do I reach it?

Hidden Kinetoscope

Patterns. That's the key.

Designers of Ages rarely do things just once, I've learned. Not Gehn, anyway. So when I sat by the spinning dome, staring at the lens in the rock, stumped after hours of exploring every nook and cranny of the area, I thought back on other secret routes I'd uncovered on these islands.

Most recently, I'd found two simply by closing the balcony doors.

Of course. I went back to the single door I'd opened to enter this dome chamber. Closing it revealed yet another secret passage. This one led directly to the hidden kinetoscope. I knew the drill by now.

Book Assembly dome symbol.

Back at the open dome, I found what I expected—another book, sealed below in a chamber. And another slider scale lock. I'm convinced these domes harbor linking books. But links to where? I know, I've asked this question before. But I'm getting no answers. A lot of puzzle pieces are in place, but I see no big picture yet.

Where's Atrus when I need him?

Is there anything that can shed light on this Age?

gehn's laboratory

My mother used to say, "Ask and you shall receive." Of course, that never worked with stuff I really wanted. But here in Riven, I've finally gotten some answers. Ironically, they're courtesy of Gehn.

Before I continue my chronicle, let me list some important things I now know or strongly suspect:

1. I believe the Star Fissure lies under the big telescope back on Temple Island!
2. Gehn has managed to create a link to another Age, where he resides and works now.
3. The rotating domes are called "Fire-marbles." They power and (as I suspected) protect the linking books to Gehn's Age.
4. I've found the five-number slider code that opens these domes!
5. That hidden building along the cliff walkway is actually Gehn's laboratory.
6. Gehn has enemies—a rebel group called the Moiety, led by Catherine, wife of Atrus. Those distinctive daggers are their calling cards.

The plot thickens.

How do I know all this? Read on.

I climbed the stairs from the Fire-marble cavern. At the balcony's double doors, I realized something was missing—a sound I'd heard earlier. This drew me back down to Gehn's frog catcher. It was quieter. I looked up.

The ventilation fan was off!

Lever on catwalk near Gehn's lab turns off ventilation fan above frog trap.

I remembered the lever back on the path, near Gehn's lab. One end of its power cable ran here, the other to Gehn's lab. Perhaps the fan ventilated the lab? Too perfect. Couldn't be. But I climbed up through the fan housing into the ventilation duct and crawled to the other end.

And here's where I ended up:

Gehn's lab. (Access through fan duct!)

This five-sided workshop is where Gehn has been trying to recreate the D'ni art of assembling and writing linking books. Arrayed neatly on work tables—inks, papers, a page press, a book binder, blank books.

Before I discuss the contents of Gehn's journal, let me point out one other important discovery. On his desk, I found the fifth wooden eye, the one with D'ni number 1 on its back. I still don't know the creature associated with it, because it emits no sound, and Gehn plucked it and brought it here. But a nearby note suggests I can see its location through a scope in what Gehn calls his "Survey Room."

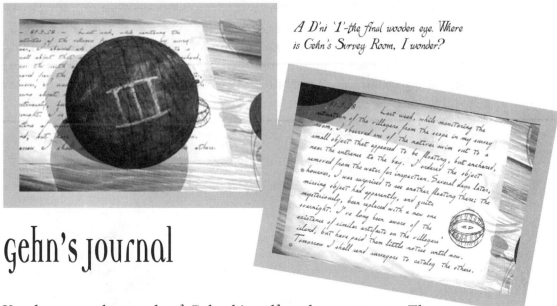

A D'ni '1'—the final wooden eye. Where is Gehn's Survey Room, I wonder?

Gehn's Journal

Yes, here are the words of Gehn himself, god among men. The guy sounds remarkably sane and thoughtful for one so feared, I must admit.

Gehn's journal–answers, at last!

The first thing I noted was his musing on "the stars beneath the Fissure"—the very phenomenon Atrus suggested I must manipulate to signal him. Gehn sealed this Fissure shut, but continues to observe its starfield. How? With a telescope, of course.

Have I seen a telescope anywhere?

The viewing device back on the Temple Island plateau, where I first arrived in Riven—could that be poised over the Star Fissure itself?

It must be!

Later:

And the revelations just keep on coming.

The most telling evidence of Gehn's basic nature comes from his primitive method of using an external source—the Fire-marble Domes—to power his crude linking books. These book repositories are stoked in turn by the massive Golden Dome. It is indeed the central power source I guessed it was.

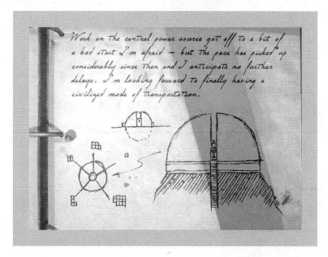

Golden Dome powers five Fire-marble Domes. Again, note grid patterns.

Dome Access code

Gehn's journal provides a five-number access code for the slider locks on the Fire-marble Domes. Unfortunately, most of the numbers are greater than 10; I don't recognize them. But they're composed of similar elements. Perhaps I can extrapolate those numbers from the ones I already know.

In another place, Gehn speaks of D'ni color symbology, concluding that entry with a six-symbol sequence—the same symbols I've been finding on the Fire-marble Domes. Perhaps he correlated each dome with a color. I must remember to seek further evidence of this.

tram car station

The view here is panoramic.

From just outside Gehn's lab I can see all three of the other main islands, including the connections—tram cables, footbridge, even the logging-car tracks rising out of the water tube. The tram just below runs directly to a strange, three-tiered island, the only one I haven't explored yet.

Surely it holds the key to Gehn's whereabouts.

View of Temple Island ((eft) and Jungle Island (right).

And there's my next destination-Survey Island.

survey island

Well, I'm getting used to the tram rides, finally. I didn't even moan this time. As the car pulled into the station, I noticed a door on the opposite (right) side of the tracks. I decided to rotate the car and check it out later, when I returned. For now, I just exited to the left, as usual.

Note that door on opposite side of tracks.

central path

I climbed to a breathtaking blue-green lagoon.

Clearly it was man-made; a grisly row of tusks at the edge somewhat tempered its beauty. Monolithic rocks sprouted from the water on either side of a winding metal walkway. Halfway up the path, an opening carved under the walkway revealed an orange-lit chamber beneath the lagoon.

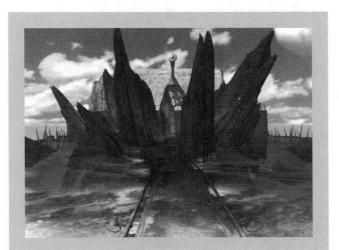

The island's lower lagoon-beautiful, but eerie.

The metal walkway ended at a stairway that climbed to a second man-made plateau. This level featured another aqua pool, dammed by a high stone wall. Huge rock islands sat in the water. From a distance, they looked natural enough. But close up, you could see rows of spigots jutting from under their rims.

What were these things?

Always keep your rock formations well-drained. It's just good hygiene.

As I write this, I sit in the shade of a trench-like path that bisects the pool. Everything feels artificial, engineered on a mammoth scale. Up ahead, a sheer rock wall rises at least 100 feet straight up.

Map viewing Balcony

Incredible. The entire second tier of the island is an immense map!

I proceeded to the rock wall, where an elevator carried me to the top. I stepped out onto a balcony, where I sit now, gawking. Trust me, it's not easy to write and gawk at the same time.

Below lies a map:

The Riven islands in miniature. Note a small fifth island at upper right. Where is it in reality?

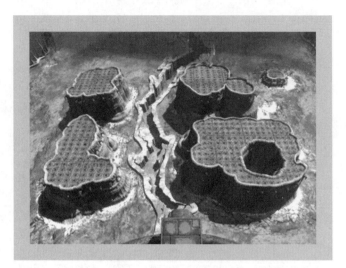

The plateau islands in the pool below depict the Riven chain. And now I understand those grid patterns from the plaque in the Golden Dome and elsewhere. Each pattern represents a Riven island. The patterns fit together to form a square, just as Riven was once a single entity.

Further proof: Buttons on a small control panel attached to the balcony railing represent the five grid patterns. When I push a button, the corresponding island below fills with weird, gelatinous Riven water that rises to form a 3-D topographical map of that island.

Before I sat to update the journal, I pushed the Temple Island button and watched it grow. Amazing. With a little of that water, I could make a name for myself back home. Why, I could set up display booths in malls all over the tricounty area.

The fire-marble dome

I could stare at maps all day, but I had Gehn to trap. And more amazing stuff lay on the other side of the elevator. Another man-made lake, for example. Here, a hundred feet above sea level! Like those below, it was rimmed with tusks.

Straight ahead, across a short gangplank, a rust-colored structure floated in the center of the lake. More on that later. But a humming to my left caught my attention. I followed it to yet another spinning Fire-marble Dome.

Survey Island Fire-marble Dome. Note its symbol—a circle with horizontal line.

It didn't take long to find the kinetoscope across the lake. But the end of its pier was warped. The scope tilted sideways; the lens didn't sight the dome symbols properly. This proved no problem, though. I just clicked wildly on the button until I nailed it. The dome retracted, glinting brilliantly in the sun.

Off-kilter kinetoscope calls for brute-force solution: Punch the button like a maniac!

3-D map chamber

Did I mention the tusk-whale totems? Wood carvings of everyone's favorite aquatic carnivore surround the rust-colored structure in the middle of the lake. I entered and approached an interesting device.

At first, I saw a simple 5-by-5 grid on the floor and another 5-by-5 grid, much smaller, on a display console with a handle. The grid pattern for Temple Island was highlighted on this console.

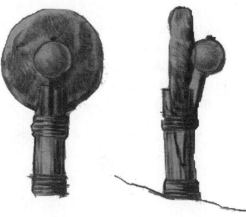

Grid pattern on control console matches active island map in lagoon.

I'd pushed the Temple Island button on the control panel overlooking the big island maps. Was this a coincidence? I thought not. Easy enough to test, though. I went back out to the balcony and pushed the Jungle Island button. Then I returned to the map chamber. Sure enough, the Jungle Island grid pattern was highlighted on the display console.

Now what? I noticed that one corner square was lit yellow. I pushed it. Suddenly, the floor grid came alive. It rose up in a 3-D topographical pin-map. It did not depict the entire Jungle Island, but only the grid section represented by the yellow-lit button on the console. It was quite detailed.

I pushed the button just below the yellow-lit one. Now *that* button glowed yellow, and its corresponding section of topography rose from the floor. The handle rotated the map, making it easy to examine from all four directions.

Cool!

Rotate map to see island features quite clearly-like, say, that Jungle Island Fire-marble Dome.

Because each square in the 5-by-5 grid on the display console was divided into its own 5-by-5 grid on the floor pin-map, the entire Riven chain could be depicted as a 25-by-25 topographical map.

I played with the map for quite a while, looking for familiar features on each island. Aside from the Temple Island Golden Dome, the most recognizable landmarks were the five Fire-marble Domes. My favorite challenge was finding the dome on Book Assembly Island. Because that Fire-marble was underground, I had to look for the tell-tale hole in the top of its cavern to pinpoint its grid location.

And I found it:

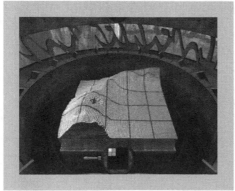

Dimple in the cliff-top-there's the Fire-marble Dome on Book Assembly Island.

Later:

Further exploration reveals little else up here. Maybe it's time to try that other door across the tram tracks.

Tram Station: Far Door

Getting across the tracks was easy; I just sat in the tram, rotated it, and stepped back out of the tram. The door was unlocked, and I entered a long passage.

At the far end, I found a spectacular orange-lit chamber—the one I'd seen from above on the first-level lagoon walkway. I pulled a nearby handle to bring a sealed elevator up through a bizarre translucent liquid. I hesitated a second, then stepped aboard.

Care for a mausoleum ride through slime? Step aboard!

underground passage

My golden elevator brought me to a long underground passage. As I followed it, I encountered a hooded fellow who found my presence disconcerting. I chased him into a nearby tram station, but he zoomed away before I could beat him up and steal all his best stuff.

Yeah, I'm big, I'm scary. Run, hood boy.

From what I remembered of Riven geography, this tram line ran directly across to Jungle Island. I returned to the passage and followed it up to perhaps the most spectacular place I'd yet seen in Riven.

Gehn's survey room

An underwater room. Actually, more like an underwater observatory. An enormous window looks out into the indigo depths of the lake. Stairs lead up to another throne-like chair laden with gadgets. Obviously, Gehn loves that kind of thing.

Could this be Gehn's Survey Room?

Gehn's made the lake his own little aquarium.

I raised the chair and brought down a wheel gadget from the right. I recognized the Fire-marble Dome symbols arrayed around the wheel on pentagonal buttons. A red bracket framed the button at the bottom of the wheel, indicating the active position.

I turned the wheel so the button with the Temple Island Fire-marble Dome symbol—a circle with a dot—was at the bottom. Then I pushed that button.

In the center viewscreen, a green bulb blinked on.

This gizmo associates dome symbols with colors.

I continued the process until I'd matched up each symbol with a color. When I lit the red bulb, I got a real treat—a visitation from a tusk-whale. He seemed to expect a handout. *Get a job!* When he swam away, I relit the red light. Sure enough, he returned. I found this amusing. I did it again. He reappeared, but gave an impatient cry. One more time, and he slammed the glass broadside in outright anger.

I enjoyed this a lot.

Sorry. No flesh for you today, pal.

Unfortunately, the color bulb for the Book Assembly Island dome symbol—circle with vertical line—had snapped off and couldn't illuminate. And I had no Fire-marble Dome symbol associated with blue or yellow. One color surely matched the dome on the tiny island shown on the map upstairs. But hadn't been there yet.

Nor did I yet grasp the overall significance of this color-association scheme. But Gehn intricately crafted these associations. They must mean something important.

I raised the color wheel and brought down the other viewer. This one had two pentagonal buttons. I pushed the left button. The viewer displayed a small, unremarkable room. I watched a moment. A woman crossed the room and then disappeared.

I won't tell you the first thought that crossed my mind. But then a more likely possibility struck me: Could this be Catherine?

Catherine in captivity?

I pushed the right-hand button and a lake appeared in the viewer. As I twirled the wheel, the view rotated: This was the shore of Village Lake back on Jungle Island! I remembered the periscope-like viewer in the water. And I remembered Gehn's note in his lab. He had seen the fifth wooden eye through his "survey scope." This was it!

A few more turns gave me the answer I needed:

Delta-shaped fish is missing creature? (Number 1 in the order.)

I'm ready now to return to Jungle Island.

The Rebel Moiety Age

I've just had the most remarkable experience. It involved drugs, but that was the bad part. So kids, don't get any wrong ideas.

I sit here in the stone pillar room, bringing these notes up to date. And I'm ready, now, to face Gehn.

All I have to do is find him.

stone pillar room (gateway to moiety age)

OK, I had my fish matched to D'ni number 1.

Thus, I knew all five creatures, and I knew the correct order. And as I worked my way back across Jungle Island, I understood with perfect clarity what this meant. The wooden eyes were a Moiety rebel code. The note in Gehn's lab made it clear the eyes mystified and concerned him. The secret tunnel behind the gallows holding cell was a Moiety construction. And the pillar-ringed cavern at the end of the tunnel was a rebel gateway.

But a gateway to what?

I entered the cavern and quickly pressed the stone pillar icons in the correct order:

Here's the gateway code, from left to right.

A water barrier drained from the far wall. Then a compartment opened, revealing a linking book. I approached and opened it. A power crystal (like the one described in Gehn's journal) framed the book's gateway image:—a dramatic landscape dominated by a gigantic spherical structure.

Without hesitation, I placed my hand on the page.

*Gateway image in the
Moiety Age linking book.*

The Moiety Age

I linked to a cave entrance, gazing out across dark waters at the Hive,
as I now call it. Spectacular, pterodactyl-like birds arced majestically
around the massive, window-pocked sphere of the structure. It sat on
the trunk of a tree. Had it grown there? An organic structure? It was
clearly inhabited. Smoke rose from a vent at the top.

*The Moiety Hive. Catherine's Age
harbors the rebel faction.*

I turned to enter the cave.

At the far end, an odd sculpted figure held a linking book. I recognized it immediately as an effigy of Gehn. Moiety-style daggers, like the ones I'd seen around the islands, sprouted from him like pins from a pincushion.

Gehn in effigy!

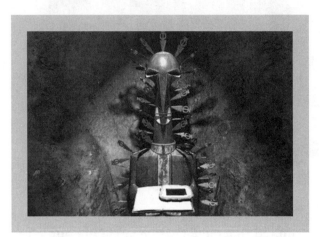

Grinning in solidarity, I stepped forward to examine it—and suddenly heard voices behind me. As I turned to look, a rebel dart lodged in my neck. Two figures approached, and all went black.

I rose briefly into consciousness. My captors rowed me across the water.

The Hive loomed ahead.

In the Moiety Hive

I awoke again on a small bench in a spare mud hut. My head throbbed; when I tried to shake out the cobwebs, I swear my brain sloshed. Whatever they put on those darts should be banned. With heroic effort, I stood and staggered across the room.

The door was locked. Was I a prisoner?

Life in the Hive–the view from my room.

My window overlooked a cluster of warmly lit huts connected by suspended walkways, much like the mud hut village on Jungle Island. But, like the Hive, these huts seemed literally to sprout from trees. Indeed, they looked like miniature versions of the great Hive.

As I turned back toward the room, I heard the door open. A woman entered. She spoke to me in another language, but I recognized Catherine's name among her first words. Then she placed a book and a slim journal on the table. It was the Prison Book Atrus had given me! She treated these objects with great respect. Then she urged me (I think) to take both, and left.

Nelah, devoted friend of Catherine.

The journal was Catherine's. It began (as does mine) shortly after her link to Riven. But tucked in the first pages was a soiled letter to me, written recently from her prison. In it, Catherine explained that someone named Nelah would return my Prison Book; now I knew the woman's name. She also pointed out that Gehn keeps a combination to her prison in his office.

Finally, she claimed to know how we might signal Atrus, but cautioned me to wait for her release.

Nelah returned the Prison Book. Now I can confront Gehn.

I continued reading her journal. I won't summarize everything, because I have much to do, myself. But she wrote of a dramatic confrontation with Gehn at the fissure, when she and Atrus managed to trap Gehn in Riven. She also mentioned the birth of the Moiety and the fracturing of the islands: "Gehn wrote this place, and it will die, as all of Gehn's Ages eventually die."

I learned much more about Gehn. But more importantly, I learned Catherine has discovered the Star Fissure. And, as I suspected, it is indeed sealed under the telescope on Temple Island—or "Allatwan," as the Moiety calls the place. Best of all, she provided the five-number combination for the locked viewport. This is entered, no doubt, by pushing the five buttons I saw on the hatch. Catherine also noted a small mechanical stop to prevent the scope from hitting the portal window.

Finally, she claimed the fissure is "as hospitable to life as a flowing river." After all, she reasoned, Atrus survived his gentle fall through its starfield.

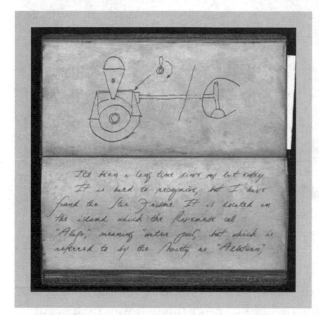

It has been a long time since my last entry. It is hard to recognize, but I have found the Star Fissure. It is located on the island which the Rivenese call "Alago," meaning "water pool," but which is referred to by the Moiety as "Aldowan."

Everything I need to know about the Star Fissure is right here in Catherine's journal.

I plunged on, reading of Gehn's crude early success at linking book creation, his use of the Fire-marbles to power them, and of Catherine's own success in creating the very Age where I now stood reading her journal. She's written a "book-window substance" into her Age, from which she creates "healing windows" to overlay the gateway images of her linking books. This frees her from any need for Gehn's clumsy domes.

One other thing:

I believe the monster I've been calling a tusk-whale is known here as a "wahrk." Catherine mentioned it only in passing, but spoke of the terror associated with this beast by the villagers.

Catherine's elegant "healing window" repairs the gateway image of her linking books.

When I finished, Nelah returned with another linking book. She opened it and set a "healing window" atop the gateway image. And I linked back here, to the cavern of stone pillars.

gehn's age

R iven is starting to feel like home. Is that good or bad? I don't
know anymore. It's a beautiful, dying world.

In any case, I worked my way back across Jungle Island to
the "frog cave" tram station in record time. Then it was off to
Temple Island. By approaching from this direction, I knew I
could access the Gate Room and use the ramp I'd raised earlier to
explore the mysterious upper level of the Golden Dome.

temple island arrival

When I arrived, I got the fright of my life.

As I approached the temple door, it slid open automatically. There, hovering like an orange nightmare in the temple imager, was the hoary head of Gehn.

Gehn's getting ahead of himself.

But as I entered, the image disappeared. It was probably triggered automatically by any temple entry.

Or so I hoped.

Golden Dome: The Marble Press

I proceeded quickly to the Gate Room, set back to its original position with the open gateway at the rear left. I stepped through the far door. The connecting ramp was still raised, just as I'd set it when I ventured over the long interisland footbridge from Book Assembly Island.

I climbed to the upper level of the Golden Dome.

I raised this ramp from the Golden Dome side many years ago, it seems. Finally, I get to use it.

Not much to see up here. Just a simple 25-by-25 grid on the floor, and a side-stand holding six marbles. Each grid square has an indentation just big enough to hold, say, a marble. Is that a clue? Nearby, a small switch lowers a massive press mechanism onto the grid. Flipping the switch also reveals a white button.

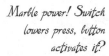

Marble power! Switch lowers press, button activates it?

When I push the white button, nothing happens.
And that's where I'm at.

Later:

I sit here at the marble press, staring. My old composition teacher always urged us to use journals as a "thinking tool." We used to laugh at him a lot. But maybe I'll give it the old college try. I can't think of any other way to work through the solution process.

I'll ask myself questions:

Q: How long would it take to solve the puzzle by randomly placing marbles on the grid?

A: Let's see. Six marbles of different colors on a 25-by-25 grid. That means, oh, about 93,850,000,000,000 possible combinations. I don't think raw power-solving is an option.

Q: Where have I encountered a 25-by-25 grid before?

A: In the Survey Island Map Chamber. OK, that's a start.

There must be some correlation here.

Q: What information did the Map Chamber grid convey?

A: Excellent follow-up question. The map grid showed me each island's key topographical features.

Q: Did any particular topographical feature stick out prominently?

A: I think so.

Q: Can you be more specific?

A: In particular, I recall the placement of the Fire-marble Domes on each island.

OK, now I'm really extracting information. I'm digging deep, I'm going for the jugular with myself. I feel myself starting to crack under the relentless pressure of myself.

Q: Do you recall the specific grid locations for each of the Fire-marble Domes?

A: No.

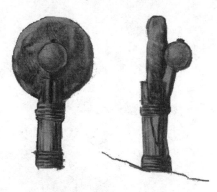

Later:

After a quick round trip to Survey Island, I have a fresh perspective. There, I drew a 25-by-25 grid on a piece of paper, manipulated the island maps, and noted the exact grid location of each Fire-marble Dome. It makes sense, doesn't it? Fire-marbles represented by marbles. Just so perfect. But now I face another problem. The marbles are different colors.

Which marble goes where?

This one's a bit easier, although it may require one small piece of guesswork.

Q: Where else have colors played a role in your sojourn across Riven?

A: In Gehn's Survey Room.

Q: How so?

A: His color wheel mechanism matched colored underwater lights with symbols on the wheel.

Q: And have those symbols matched up with anything else in Riven?

A: Each symbol has been associated with a particular Fire-marble Dome.

Symbol	Color	Dome on Island
	Blue	Prison
	Green	Temple
	Yellow	None
	Orange	Survey
	Red	Jungle
	(Broken)	Book Assembly

Well, not *each* symbol. I haven't seen the symbol on the tiny fifth island yet. And the underwater light for the Book Assembly Island dome symbol was broken. But I know enough that I can make an educated guess.

Later:

Success! It took some experimentation, but not much. Here's a shot of the successful marble array before I lowered the press.

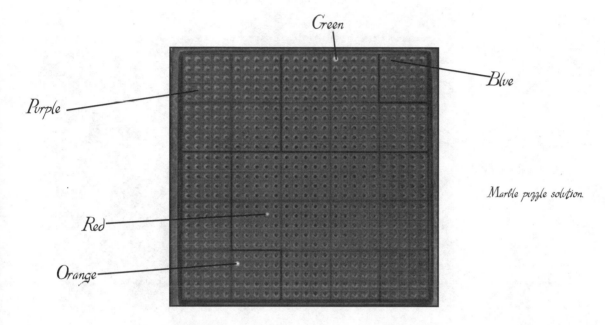

Marble puzzle solution.

When the press came down, a powerful blast of wind indicated a tremendous surge of power from the Golden Dome. Surely all five Fire-marble Domes are fully powered up now. I'll just head straight for the one here on Temple Island.

fire-marble dome (Temple island)

Easier said than done. I had to do some fancy rotating from the main antechamber of the Gate Room to get out the rear-right gate. Then I went through. (Thank goodness I'd opened the outer door earlier, when I crossed the interisland bridge from Book Assembly Island.) I followed the catwalk around into the Golden Dome. From there, it was easy to work my way back down to the open Fire-marble.

Am I ready for Gehn?

As I approached the slider lock, I pulled out both the access code from Gehn's lab journal. I also took the Prison Book from my camera case. If I was linking to Gehn's Age, I knew it would be the only ally (or weapon?) I'd have.

How to Translate D'ni Numbers Greater Than 10

If I want this to be a thorough chronicle, I should mention how I deciphered the access code. When I first saw the code in Gehn's lab journal, I didn't recognize most of the numbers. But the way the symbol patterns changed logically at 5 and 10 helped me figure out the other D'ni numbers.

Here's how:

The D'ni number for 5, I noticed, is simply a D'ni 1 rotated one turn to the left. The D'ni 6 combines the D'ni 5 symbol with a D'ni 1 symbol. The D'ni 7 combines 5 and 2; D'ni 8 combines 5 and 3; and D'ni 9 combines 5 and 4. Finally, D'ni 10 is a D'ni 2 rotated one turn left.

This pattern continues up to 25. The D'ni 15 is a D'ni 3 rotated one turn left, and D'ni 20 is a D'ni 4 rotated left one turn. Thus, the D'ni numbers from 1 to 24 are as follows:

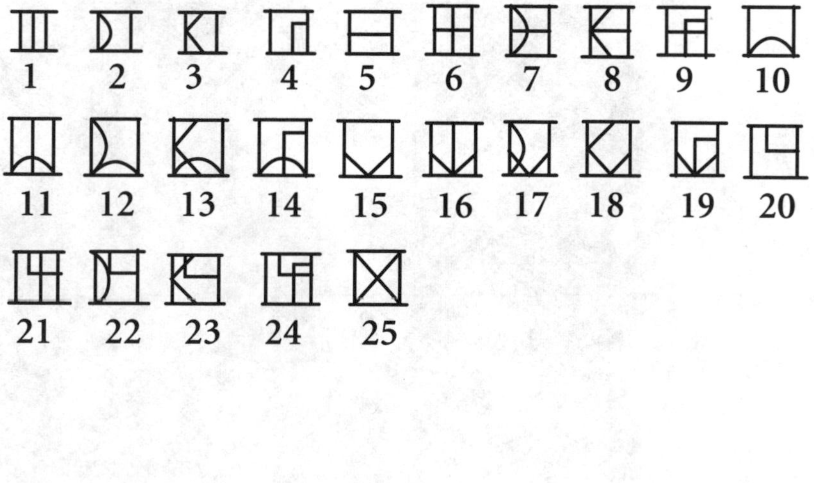

1	2	3	4	5	6	7	8	9	10

11	12	13	14	15	16	17	18	19	20

21	22	23	24	25

Although D'ni number symbology derives from fives, it is in fact a Base 25 number system. Numbers from 1 to 25 are represented by a single symbol, or digit. After 25, you add a second digit; the number (1 to 25) in the second-digit position actually represents a multiple of 25 (just as the number in the second-digit position in our Base 10 represents a multiple of 10).

For example, the symbol for Gehn's Age, is a two-digit number that translates to 98. But that's not the 98 we know from our Base 10. It's actually 9 sets of 25 (or 225 in Base 10) plus 8 more units. Thus, Gehn's Age is his 233rd.

OK, enough math.

I moved the slider bars to the numbers on the scale that matched the five-number code. As the outer dome closed over me, the inner dome slid open. The book podium rose from the floor, and there it was—the linking book to Gehn's 233rd Age. I opened the book and saw a desolate landscape in the gateway image. Then I placed my hand on the page.

The link to Gehn's Age. Cheery, isn't it?

gehn's office

At last. Gehn. Master of the monologue.

I can't say I particularly dislike the man. He was pleasant enough, and seemed genuinely repentant of his past sins, to which he freely confessed. He admitted having tried to murder his own son, and said, "I have changed." But then he tried to justify his actions by adding, "My mission was an honorable one."

Interesting.

Gehn: The man, the myth.

Gehn is particularly disturbed, I can tell, by Catherine. He sees her as a fundamental rival now, clearly. His no-nonsense directive to refrain from any attempt to free Catherine was most emphatic. He claims Atrus is unaware of "what she has become," as he delicately put it.

Then we got down to business. He asked to examine my false linking book. When he saw D'ni in its window, he started. He flipped pages intently, then flipped back to the gateway image. I could see it was a great struggle for him to keep from slapping his hand hard onto the page. But caution got the better of him—exactly as Catherine predicted in her letter.

He approached and asked me to go through first. I had him right where Atrus wanted him.

And then I chickened out.

That's right. I blinked.

It was stupid, I'll admit. It can only fuel his suspicion to have me hesitate like that. But I just couldn't do it. Put my hand on a trap? What if Gehn didn't follow? Did I really want to run the risk of spending the rest of my life as a footnote?

Who do I trust?

Gehn was disappointed, I knew, but he masked it well. He powered up his linking books and offered me free access to the Riven islands. Donning goggles and gloves, he reiterated his desire to resolve matters with Atrus—"especially in light of what Catherine has become." He warned me not to signal him unless I decided to use the book; he added that the call switch would reset itself once I link from here.

And now I sit here in a cage, pondering my next move.

Later:

I linked away to reset the button, and then linked back immediately. I pushed the call button and watched Gehn approach. He acted pleased to see me, and offered the Prison Book once again. This time I put out my hand quickly—too quickly, I feared. But I didn't want to miss another opportunity.

All went dark as I linked into what seemed like pure nothingness.

For a moment I felt lost, abandoned. Had I been duped? By Atrus, Gehn, everyone? I felt a deep pity for Sirrus and Achenar, Atrus's sons long imprisoned in trap books like this one. I couldn't imagine a worse fate, really—locked in a black void with nothing but your own fevered thoughts to accompany you.

But then the book's cover lifted.

And there was Gehn.

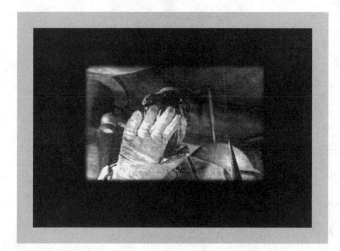

Fortunately, Gehn is a hands-on kind of guy.

It didn't take him long to follow. He took his gun with him, I noticed.

Atrus was right.

I ended up in his office, outside the bars. Knowing Gehn was gone for good left me feeling pleased. But then I remembered Riven's fragile state. The Fifth Age could collapse at any moment. Catherine would perish, and I'd be stuck forever in this godforsaken hellhole.

Gehn's music player.

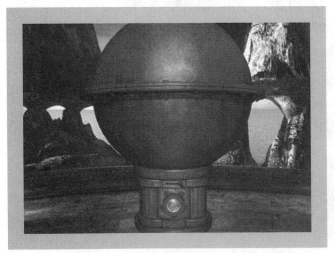

This furnace-like device powers up Gehn's Riven island linking books.

Gehn's desk.

Catherine's letter said I'd need a combination to release her, so I'd better start looking.

Gehn's Bedroom

I found nothing resembling a lock combination in Gehn's office. But Gehn's bedroom featured several items of interest.

First, I found another imager with a brief message from a delightful young woman who, I learned, was Gehn's wife. I also found his personal journal. It merely confirmed my feelings about the man. Condescension and brutality are there in equal parts; corrupted by his power and knowledge, Gehn is blinded by the perceived glories of his D'ni civilization. His Rivenese subjects are entirely expendable, and his disdain for Atrus is powerful.

Images of Gehn's wife, Keta.

Clearly, though, the man has suffered pain. Apparently, he'd lost his father in some horrible way. And the woman in the imager was his wife, Keta. She, too, is gone now. Perhaps Gehn has a right to his bitterness. Perhaps not.

In any case, he's clearly a dangerous man.

Later:

I think I've found the "combination" I seek. It took a link to Prison Island to figure it out, but I got back easily and now plan to jot it down.

It's a sound code. I should have known. The globe watch on Gehn's nightstand makes a sequence of five sounds when opened. There are only three different sounds—a ding, a click, and a kind of *whirrr*—that combine in a sequence of five to form the combination.

Catherine's prison combination-listen carefully!

Once I got it down, I climbed back up to the office and went to the Prison Island linking book. I'm truly looking forward to meeting Catherine, goddess of the Rebel Moiety, at last.

Gehn's linking book to
Prison Island

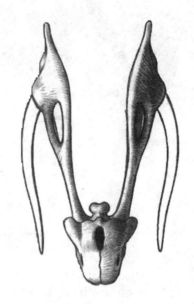

prison island

Prison Island. Incarceration never looked so lovely. It's small, but beautiful, in an Alcatraz sort of way.

This was once the Great Tree, as I know from Catherine's journal. I can see that. Really, that's one *big* stump. Reminds me of the giant redwood on Myst Island, only bigger—much, much bigger.

Prison Island

Now that I have a moment, let me tell you what happened on my first trip here. I arrived in the island's Fire-marble Dome chamber, as I expected. The only path led to a caged elevator. I yanked the handle and rode up. And there she was.

Catherine, wife of Atrus, goddess of the Moiety, bane of Gehn.

My presence caught Catherine off-guard.

"You made it!" she said, pleased. "But how did you get past—?"

She stopped abruptly. Quickly composing herself, she changed her tone. Her eyes flicked up at a spot above my head, and then I remembered—the spy apparatus in Gehn's Survey Room.

She leaned close and whispered. The elevator combination, she reminded me, was somewhere in Gehn's office. And then she backed away with feigned disdain.

"Go then!" she commanded. "If you won't help me, then I have nothing more to say."

I nearly applauded. *Oscar time!*

As the elevator hit bottom, I carefully examined the lock control apparatus. It was a sound-key device. Three keys, three small sounds. Diabolically simple. I pressed each key several times to memorize the sounds. Then I headed back for my final confrontation with Gehn, knowing what I needed to find in his office.

Sound keys, left to right—click, whirrr, ding.

Later:

The code worked perfectly. As the cage bars slid aside, a powerful feeling of anticipation gripped me. Gehn was trapped; Catherine was free. Only one thing remained—the signal to Atrus.

As I descended the elevator with Catherine, she directed me to the Star Fissure plateau. At the bottom, I let her link off Prison Island first; she needed time to gather her villagers and link them to safety in the Rebel Moiety Age. After she left, I had to reset the Fire-marble Dome. But that was simple enough now.

Then, after reopening the inner dome with the slider code and linking back to Gehn's office, I used his Temple Island linking book to begin what I hoped was the final leg of this journey.

Gehn's linking book to Temple Island.

The star fissure

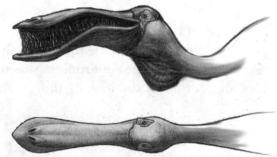

And now the moment of truth.

      I know that sounds portentous. But I do want to help these people. *And* I want to get back home in one piece: I don't wish to become a martyr for the Cause. I'm not even sure what "the Cause" is.

  It didn't take long to reach the Star Fissure telescope. I had to lower the ramp between the Golden Dome and the Gate Room, but aside from that, the way was clear and straightforward. When I reached the telescope, I rechecked the viewport hatch combination in Catherine's journal.

Then I crouched to the hatch on the ground.

Mentally numbering the buttons 1 to 5 from left to right, I entered the combination and opened the viewport.

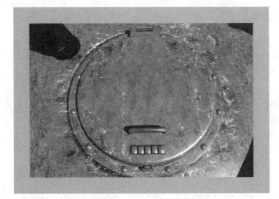

Five-number combination from Catherine's journal unlocks the Star Fissure viewport.

I stepped back and peeked through the eyepiece. Yes, that's a Star Fissure, all right.

I crouched again to see the "small mechanical stop" mentioned in Catherine's journal. It was on the left strut. I pulled up the handle to retract the locking pin.

Handle on strut retracts locking pin.

I stepped back again and pulled down the power valve at right to activate the telescope mechanism. Then I pushed the button near the handle to lower the telescope. Knowing Gehn, it would take five increments of movement to penetrate the portal. So after the fourth push, I stopped.

Lever at right routes power to telescope, button lowers it to viewport.

I looked around, taking in Riven's beauty one last time. Was I about to destroy it?

What power would I unleash?

I pushed the button a fifth time.

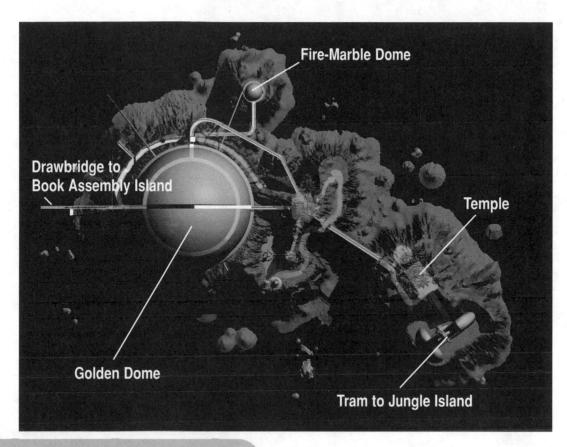

Fire-Marble Dome

Drawbridge to
Book Assembly Island

Temple

Golden Dome

Tram to Jungle Island

chapter one

Temple Island

Game Opening: Prison Escape

Riven opens by caging you. Isn't that just so appropriate? But after the prison guard relieves you of the Prison Book Atrus gave you, a disguised intruder—a Moiety rebel, to be precise—disables the guard with a blowgun dart, grabs the Prison Book, and proceeds to liberate you. As the cage lowers, you're left staring at an odd mechanism.

Odd mechanisms in *Riven*? What a shock.

Note
This opening location, Temple Island, is a central connecting point to other islands. You can't solve all of its puzzles just yet. Instead, you return in later chapters.

◆ First things first. Open Atrus's journal in your inventory and read *everything*. Learn about Gehn (Atrus's father), Riven's deterioration, the fate of Catherine (Atrus's wife), the mysterious Star Fissure, and the Prison Book Atrus gave you—the very book you lost to the prison guard, then to your liberator.

◆ Move forward to the odd mechanism.

◆ Examine the mechanism. It's some sort of viewing device, pointing down at a round plate on the floor. None of the controls work yet. You must direct power to the device first.

◆ Turn around and go back toward the prison cell you just escaped.

◆ At the cell, turn left and follow the path up the stairs.

◆ At the top of the stairs, turn left and enter the room. This is a Gate Room antechamber. Up ahead is a doorway with a big button on the wall to the right.

The Gate Room puzzle

The Gate Room is a pentagonal inner chamber that rotates within a circular outer wall. Two of the inner chamber's five sides have open doorways—the one you just came through and one across the room. The outer wall has five gateways, but two are blocked by lowered gates, including the one you must get through to continue exploring.

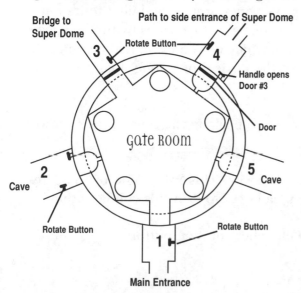

To rotate the inner chamber: Push any chamber rotation button just outside four of the five gateways. One push rotates the chamber one-fifth of a turn. Your task: Rotate the inner chamber to find switches to raise the two lowered gates. Then rotate again to access the escape gate.

From the start position, do the following:

◆ Push the chamber rotation button right of the door four times.

◆ This rotates the inner chamber four-fifths of a full turn.

◆ Turn around and exit the antechamber.

◆ Turn left and go forward four times down the stairs.

◆ Turn left twice to face a locked gate.

◆ Click beneath the gate for a close-up; then click again to slip under and enter the dark spooky chamber.

◆ Click on the ladder to climb. At the top, continue forward across the plank into the Gate Room. Aha!

◆ Cross the Gate Room and enter the cave through the far doorway.

◆ Approach and click on the small lever.

The symbol on the lever gives you a pretty good clue to its function. Pulling this lever opens a steam valve that sends hydraulic power to the strange, cone-shaped viewing device you examined just outside your prison cell. You won't use the device for a long, long time, but what the heck. Give it power!

◆ Turn around and take two steps back up the cave to the position just outside the Gate Room.

◆ Pull the lever left of the doorway. This raises one of the gates inside. Unfortunately, you can't get to it in this configuration.

◆ Turn right and push the chamber rotation button.

◆ Push the button again.

◆ Enter the Gate Room and go through the doorway (and the now-open gate) into another outer chamber. Oops. A big locked door blocks your exit.

◆ Turn back to the doorway and pull the lever left of the door. This raises the other gate inside.

◆ Turn right and push the chamber rotation button.

◆ Push the button again.

◆ Cross the Gate Room and go to the chamber rotation button just outside the other open door. (This is where you originally entered.)

◆ Push this chamber rotation button twice. This returns the inner chamber to its original configuration.

◆ Cross the room and go through the now-open doorway.

◆ Cross the bridge and enter the massive domed building.

The Golden Dome

No, you haven't completely solved the Gate Room puzzle yet. Notre Dame fans should perk up here, however. Yes, you're in a really big Golden Dome. Inside you'll find some catwalks and hydraulic levers. One important lever is at the entrance; you can see it if you turn around just inside the dome doorway. No power is routed to it yet, so leave it alone for now.

◆ Take two steps forward across the catwalk.

◆ Click on the wall plaque at the bottom of the screen (on the cat-walk railing.) The plaque shows you that power pipes from this golden dome lead to five different locations, each designated by a grid pattern.

◆ Go left down the catwalk. Continue along the stairs that wind halfway around the dome.

◆ Follow the catwalk outside to the hissing pipe.

◆ Examine the diagram on the pipe. Looks like it powers some sort of bridge.

◆ Click on the small lever to open the steam valve.

Opening this valve sends steam power to the drawbridge on the west end of the island. If you turn left and look up, you can see how the pipe runs to the raised drawbridge. This bridge connects Book Assembly Island to the Golden Dome. You won't use it now, though. In this walkthrough, we get to Book Assembly Island a different way. (From there, we come back here to lower the drawbridge and return to the Golden Dome. See "Connect Book Assembly Island to Golden Dome" in "Book Assembly Island.")

◆ Return to the main catwalk and continue left around the dome.

◆ Go through the dark cave to another pipe.

◆ Again, examine the diagram on the pipe. Another drawbridge power-up, apparently.

◆ Click on the small lever to open the steam valve.

Yes, opening this valve sends steam power to another drawbridge that runs *east* from the Golden Dome, connecting it with the Gate Room. Again, you won't use it now. But it's powered up for later use. This is a good thing. Let satisfaction course through your veins for a moment. OK, that's enough. You have a *long* way to go.

◆ Return to the Golden Dome.

◆ Go back up the stairs to the dome entrance. (Pull the lever there to see the drawbridge operate. Pull the lever again to relower the bridge.)

◆ Cross the bridge to return to the Gate Room.

◆ Exit the Gate Room through the far door.

◆ Cross the footbridge to the Temple.

Throne Room

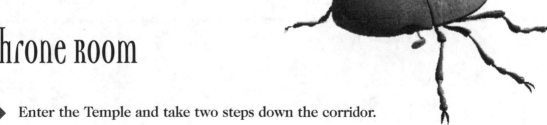

◆ Enter the Temple and take two steps down the corridor.

◆ Turn left and click on the door to open it.

◆ Enter the room. The door shuts behind you.

◆ Click on the throne-like chair to raise the cage around it.

◆ Step once toward the throne; then turn right to see a viewing device on the wall.

◆ Click on the device for a close-up. You see a room lined with pillars.

- Click on the switch next to the viewing device. On the viewscreen, watch a door open. Let's go find that door, shall we?

- Exit the throne room.

- Turn left and follow the corridor to the end.

- Open the stone door and enter the chamber.

gehn's temple

- Explore the chamber.

- Exit through the open door at the end of the column of pillars. (This is the same door you saw open in the viewscreen up in the throne room.)

tram station

- Approach the device at the bottom of the short staircase.

- Click on the blue button atop the sphere—a tram call. Watch the car approach.

- Enter the tram car.

- Click on the knob at left to pull it right and rotate the car 180 degrees.

Click on the center lever to activate the car. Enjoy the ride.

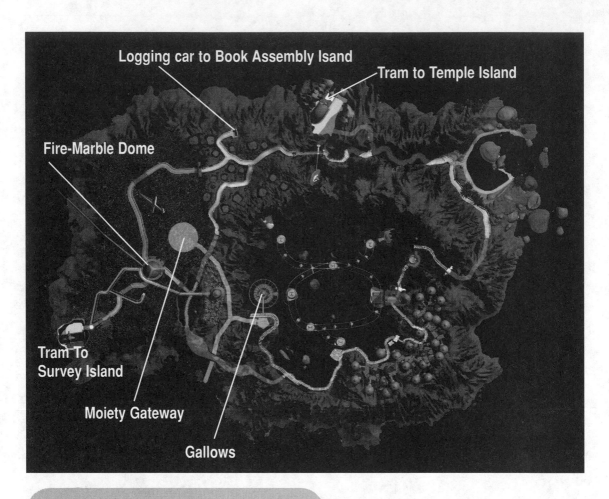

Logging car to Book Assembly Isand

Tram to Temple Island

Fire-Marble Dome

Tram To
Survey Island

Moiety Gateway

Gallows

jungle island

This island of Riven features a central lake surrounded by cliffs, a spectacular rain forest on the west end of the island (hence its name), a gorgeous lagoon to the east, and a cluster of simple mud dwellings in the southeast.
After you arrive, turn left and exit the car.

Arrival Area

◆ Move forward to the wall and turn right.

◆ Click on the small round object for a close-up. Looks like a wooden eye, doesn't it?

◆ Click on the eye. Note the symbol on the back and the frog-like chirping sound. (This will be important later.)

The symbol on the back of the wooden eye is actually a D'ni numeral, one of several you'll find throughout Riven. Elsewhere on Jungle Island you'll find information for translating these numerals.

◆ Turn around and enter the cave opening.

◆ Go forward once to climb halfway up the stairs.

◆ Turn around and look back at the cave opening.

Does that look like a frog, or what? And note where the wooden eye is located in the frog outline—right where the eye would be on an actual frog. Weird! Could it be a bizarre coincidence? Or is there some shadowy master design? How many stupid rhetorical questions can we ask *in one paragraph?*

◆ Turn around and climb the spiraling rock stairs to the cave opening.

◆ When you reach the cave opening, turn around and note the tram call at left. You'll return to use it later in the game.

◆ Exit the cave.

◆ Descend the stone stairway (lower left) until you see the "sunners" (seal-like animals) on the rocks.

◆ *Stop!*

◆ Don't move forward until the sunners stop moving!

sunner rock

Sunners are wonderful creatures. They're communal, loving, and highly intelligent, not unlike dolphins.

◆ Wait until the sunners lower their heads.

◆ Take a step onto the beach. (If you approach the sunners while their heads are up, you spook them and they slip away.)

◆ One of the sunners barks a warning. Note the sound for later.

◆ As you face Sunner Rock, turn right and follow the beach, skirting the lagoon.

◆ Go as far as possible; then turn left.

◆ Look at the rocks in the lagoon.

These rocks form the outline of another creature. Looks kind of like a whale, doesn't it? Actually, it's a deadly wahrk, an aquatic cross between whale and shark. Wahrks are brutal, efficient killers with a taste for human flesh. Note that another wooden eye is lodged in the left end of the rock formation.

◆ Click anywhere on the rock to get a close-up of the wooden eye.

◆ Click on the eye to see another symbol and hear the odd wahrk's cry. Note both for later. Again, the symbol is a D'ni numeral. We'll translate it later. Follow the beach back to the path and go left.

◆ Follow the path to the stairs and climb them to the tunnel.

◆ Continue through the lighted tunnel.

village lake

◆ When you reach the other end of the tunnel, you hear a warning alarm sound. A guard in a sentry post signals to someone below and disappears.

◆ Proceed across the wooden walkway to the end.

◆ Look down to see the ladder below you.

◆ Climb down the ladder and approach the dry basin.

◆ Click on the spigot at lower right to fill the basin.

◆ Look at the shape of the water in the basin. Looks kind of bug-like. And there's another wooden eye!

◆ Click on the wooden eye for a close-up.

◆ Rotate the eye to see the D'ni number symbol and hear the weird rubbing, clicking sound. Again, note them for later.

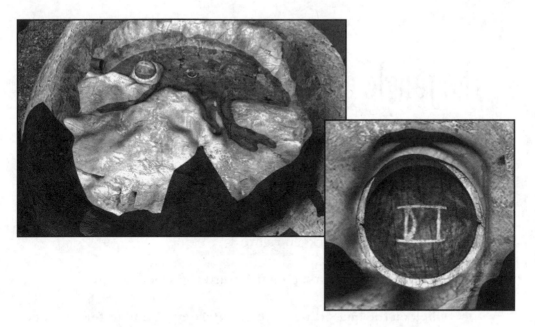

At this point, you could go past the basin, and then climb down and explore until you reach a dead end. But *what* a dead end. It's a shimmering hole in the water! Next to those Senate Campaign Finance hearings, this is just about the wildest, most fascinating thing I've ever seen. You can't go down into the water hole yet, so return to the bug basin.

◆ From the bug basin, climb the ladder and go back all the way past Sunner Rock to the stone stairs.

◆ Climb the stairs. (Climb past the cave on the right that leads to the tram station.)

◆ At the top, cross the wood-and-rope suspension bridge and continue down the path past the tree stumps.

The jungle path

◆ Somebody did some serious logging around here. Entire *hills* have been clear-cut. But it makes sense; books are big in Riven, particularly strategy guides. Wood pulp is a precious commodity, as you'll learn soon enough.

◆ At the first path fork, go right.

◆ At the next path fork, go left toward the wooden gate.

◆ Click on the bug sitting on the right gatepost and note the sound. Aha!

◆ Same noise as the wooden eye in the bug-shaped pool.

◆ Click on the gate to open it.

◆ Go through the gate and follow the path through the forest.

◆ Continue down the stairs—you hear a deep rumbling—and through a tree trunk. You see a bunch of cool blue phosphorescent stuff growing near the path.

◆ Turn left and spot the gigantic dagger stuck in the ground. Approach it and follow the rough steps down to another wooden eye.

◆ Click on the eye to hear the sound of a sunner bark. Again, note the D'ni number symbol on the back.

◆ Return to the main path.

◆ At the Y-fork, go right.

◆ Follow the path until the music gets spooky again and you see the big wahrk idol.

The wahrk idol

◆ Note the two decorative lampposts in front of the idol.

◆ When facing the idol, click on the top of the right lamppost to flip a hidden switch. The idol's mouth opens.

◆ Enter the idol's mouth and climb the stairs to the elevator. Note the blue tram call button in front of the elevator.

◆ Enter the elevator.

Inside the elevator, you can drag the handle at right to its bottom position to ride down one level. This leads to a tram station that connects Jungle Island to Survey Island. However, you needn't use the tram from here in this walkthrough.

◆ Drag the handle at right to its topmost position to ride the elevator up one level.

◆ Exit and proceed along a high jungle catwalk. (Reminds you *Myst* fans of Channelwood, doesn't it?)

◆ At the fork where you see the spinning dome, take the left fork and continue to the end.

fire-marble Dome (jungle island)

◆ Examine the spinning Fire-marble Dome and note its location next to a rumbling volcanic fissure.

◆ Go back to the path fork and turn left. Take that fork to the spinning device (a "kinetoscope").

◆ Click on the eyepiece to view a series of symbols on the kinetoscope.

◆ When the yellow-highlighted symbol appears, click quickly on the button at the top of the eyepiece.

This can be tricky. You must be quick. But you'll nail it eventually; the kinetoscope stops spinning, as does the Fire-marble Dome. For a brief moment you can see a linking book, but then an inner seal slides shut. Note the yellow-highlighted symbol for later use. Here, it's a horizontal eye with a vertical line.

◆ Return to the Fire-marble Dome via the other fork of the catwalk and look inside to see the slider puzzle. Obviously, you need more information to solve the slider puzzle and access the dome.

◆ Turn around, exit the dome, and turn left.

◆ Climb the stairs to the tower surrounded by pillars.

gehn's watchtower

◆ Click on the tower door to open it. Then enter the tower.

◆ Click on the throne to sit.

◆ Click on the left handle to activate the throne. The chair rotates and rises.

◆ Look down on the lake. Note the amazing water holes and the underwater track. Note also the cage-like platform directly below the throne.

◆ Click on the throne's right handle to close the bottom of the cage-like platform.

◆ Click on the left handle to lower the chair.

◆ Open the door and exit the tower.

◆ Follow the walkway back to the elevator.

◆ Enter the elevator and drag the handle down to its middle position.

◆ Ride down one level. Then pull the lever at left to open the wahrk idol's mouth.

◆ Exit the idol and follow the path; you see a child who runs from you.

◆ Continue to the fork in the cave under the Fire-marble Dome.

◆ Take the right fork, climb the glowing red stairway, and go through the wooden gate to the next intersection.

◆ Turn right and follow the precarious catwalk into an eerie, blue-lit cave.

◆ Halfway down the cave stairs, turn left to see the glyph of a god-like creature feeding people to hungry wahrks. Creepy!

◆ Continue down the wooden walkway as it winds around Village Lake.

◆ As you near the village, you'll see the child again. Her mother appears to bustle her off to safety.

The village

◆ Keep following the walkway to the ladder.

◆ Climb ladders and cross the plank to the dried mud dwelling.

◆ Try the star-shaped knocker until a face appears. Then back away from the door.

◆ Move down the walkway to the left.

◆ Climb the ladder and continue along the walkway to the big metal contraption—a submarine.

village dock

◆ Push the lever at left to lower the submarine into the lake. Yes, that's all you do here.

◆ Retrace your route back to the front of the mud dwelling. Note the submarine below, sitting on underwater tracks.

◆ Climb down the ladder and retrace your route all the way back along the lake, then through the eerie, blue-lit cave.

◆ After you emerge from the cave, follow the footbridge past the wooden gate on your left.

◆ Climb the stairs and exit the forest into the cleared area full of stumps.

◆ Go right at the intersection and continue across the suspension bridge.

◆ Continue past Sunner Rock and through the tunnel to the bug-shaped basin with the wooden eye.

◆ Continue past the basin, climb down the ladder, and follow the walkway to the next ladder.

◆ Enter the tunnel and climb down the ladder into the submarine.

◆ Click the center handle to turn the sub around.

◆ Click the right handle to move forward to the juncture.

◆ Be sure the bottom handle is to the right, so that you take the right-hand track. (It should be, already.)

◆ Click the right handle again to move forward a second time. You arrive at the Dock Ramp Control Tower.

◆ Look up and click to open the hatch.

◆ Climb the ladder to exit the submarine.

◆ Turn around to face the rungs in the wall.

Dock Ramp control Tower

◆ Approach the rungs and look up. Wow. That's a long climb.

◆ Climb the rungs to the room at the top of the tower.

◆ Step forward to the levers.

You find five levers in the control tower room. These control the access ramps at the five submarine docks around the lake. Moving a lever to the up position extends the ramp at the corresponding dock.

◆ Flip all five levers to the up position.

◆ Climb back down the ladder to the submarine.

◆ Click the center handle to turn the sub around.

◆ Click the right handle to go forward to the next juncture.

◆ Click the bottom handle to slide it left and select the left track.

◆ Click the right handle to go forward again.

village schoolroom

◆ Exit the submarine and turn around.

◆ Go to the door of the house-like structure and open it.

◆ Enter the schoolroom and step forward once.

◆ Turn left and click on the "hangman" device for a close-up.

◆ Click on the ring on the base at right to activate the device.

◆ Note the selected symbol, and then count the number of clicks as the hanging figure lowers toward the carnivorous wahrk.

◆ Keep playing, matching each symbol to the number of clicks to learn D'ni numbers from 1 to 10.

Wait, I forgot. You don't have to figure out anything. Take a peek below at the D'ni numbers you're supposed to learn in school. (Just don't tell the teacher I let you cheat off my paper, OK?) But that's not all. Cheat Boy isn't finished yet. To solve a later puzzle, you need to know D'ni numerals from 11 to 25, too. D'ni numbers higher than 10 combine symbols of previous numbers in an ingenious (or nefarious, depending on your outlook) way.

Here are the D'ni numerals from 1 to 25:

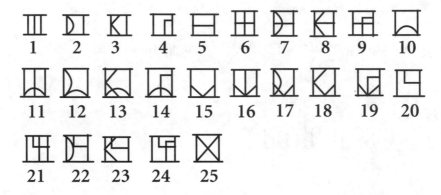

Decoding D'ni numbers tells you those symbols on the back of the wooden eyes are actually numerals. The bug eye is 2, the frog eye is 3, the sunner eye is 4, and the wahrk eye is 5. So there appears to be an order to the creatures. What creature is number 1, I wonder? Let's be on the lookout.

Here's a bonus translation of the D'ni writing on the blackboard—"The Rules of Gehn: Gehn is our master, Gehn created us, Gehn defeated Atrus."

◆ Return to the submarine.

◆ Click the center handle to turn around.

◆ Click the right handle to go forward once.

◆ Be sure the bottom handle is still in the left position to select the left track.

◆ Click the right handle to go forward again.

wahrk gallows

The rest of the steps in Jungle Island lead to a place—the gateway to the Moiety Age—that you won't know how to access yet. (Unless you really cheat and look ahead to that Age.) But because we're here on Jungle Island, let's learn how to access that gateway. It may save time later.

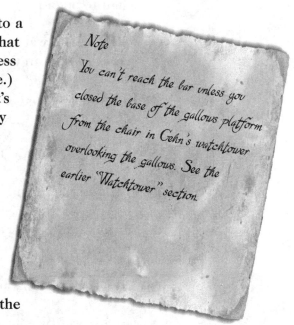

Note

You can't reach the bar unless you closed the base of the gallows platform from the chair in Gehn's watchtower overlooking the gallows. See the earlier "Watchtower" section.

◆ Exit the submarine, turn around, and go to the center of the gallows.

◆ Click on the small, triangle-shaped handle. This lowers a bar on a rope.

◆ Click on the bar to ride to the top of the gallows.

Holding cell and Rebel tunnel

◆ Move forward across the plank to the cage with the prisoner.

◆ Turn right and follow the walkway to the star-shaped control button on the rock wall.

◆ Click on the button for a close-up, and then click again to open the cage.

◆ Go back to the cage. Where's the prisoner?

◆ Enter the cage and click on the floor grate for a close-up; click again to open it.

◆ Click on the water in the grate. You pull up a ring that opens a secret passage in the cage's back wall.

◆ Enter the tunnel. The door slides shut behind you. Darkness reigns! But don't panic. I'm here for you, man.

◆ Be brave. Go forward eight times through the darkness.

◆ Click on the handle at left to illuminate a light bulb.

◆ Turn around, go forward to the next light bulb, and click on it to turn it on, too.

◆ Take one step forward and click on the next light.

◆ Go forward two steps and click on the next light.

◆ Turn around and click on the handle at the right to swing a door across the passage, revealing another corridor.

◆ Follow the corridor to the pillar room.

stone pillar gateway

This room contains 25 stone pillars, each etched with an animal icon. Experiment by clicking on a few. Your task here is to click on five in the correct order to access another age. Four of the symbols look familiar—bug, frog, sunner, wahrk—and you know the numbers associated with those four, so you know the correct order to click on them. But you don't yet know the creature symbol associated with 1, the first in the order. Let's go find it.

◆ Exit the stone pillar gateway.

◆ Go back up the corridor to the secret door.

◆ Pull the ring on the floor at lower right to open the secret door.

◆ Go through the cage.

◆ Turn right and follow the walkway down to the ladder.

◆ Click on the ladder to lower it.

◆ Climb down the ladder.

◆ Turn around and follow the walkway around the Village Lake and up through the eerie, blue-lit tunnel.

◆ Continue forward past the wooden gate, up the stairs, and out of the forest.

Logging car to Book assembly island

◆ At the first intersection, go left.

◆ At the next intersection, go right.

◆ Board the logging car and push the handle at left.

◆ Enjoy your wild roller-coaster ride through the water tunnel to Book Assembly Island. It's great fun.

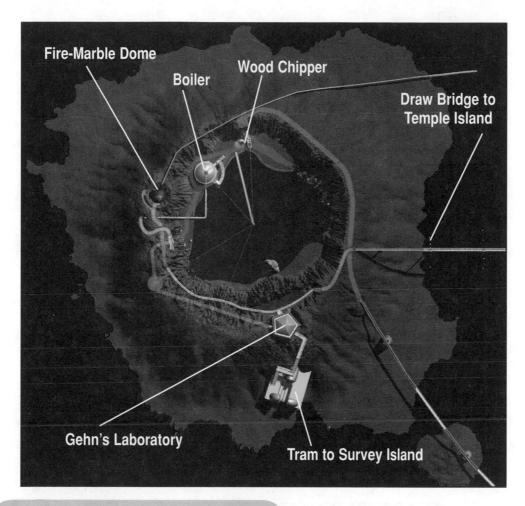

Fire-Marble Dome

Boiler

Wood Chipper

Draw Bridge to
Temple Island

Gehn's Laboratory

Tram to Survey Island

book assembly island

Welcome to Book Assembly Island, home of the most aromatic frogs you'll ever smoke. Gehn's laboratory is hidden here, too. Your logging car ride ends with you getting dumped into a wood chipper. Fortunately, the thing's not on. It would be unpleasant to be chipped.

wood chipper

◆ Climb down the ladder from the wood chipper.

◆ Turn right and take two steps forward to the pier that extends into the lake.

◆ Follow the pier to the valve control handle.

central valve controls

This control valve has three settings. (*Myst* fans, remember the water pumps in the Stoneship Age?) If you look around, you can see where the pipes go from the valve. Left position powers the wood chipper, middle powers the boiler, and right powers an interesting device by Gehn's laboratory.

To Frog Trap

To Wood Chipper

To Boiler

◆ For now, click and drag the valve handle to the middle position to power the boiler.

◆ Exit the pier and turn left.

◆ Move down the beach to the large structure—yes, the boiler.

wood chip boiler controls

◆ Climb the stairs to the walkway that runs around the boiler.

◆ Follow the walkway to the boiler control lever on the left.

◆ Make sure the lever on the Y-valve is pushed out away from you. This directs power to the boiler's water pump.

◆ Turn right to face the main controls.

Water Level Control

Boiler Grate Control

Furnace Control

◆ Click on the handle at lower right (moving it up) to turn off the boiler furnace. (You should see the water stop boiling in the glass view slot.)

◆ Click on the wheel valve at left to lower the water level. (You should see the water level drop in the glass view slot.)

◆ Turn left and click on the Y-valve lever to pull it toward you. This routes power to the boiler grate mechanism.

◆ Turn right and click on the switch at upper right. (You should see the boiler grate rise in the glass view slot.)

◆ Go back to the boiler door. The red light at right should be off.

◆ Open the door and enter the boiler.

Boiler pipe passage

◆ Approach the drain in the center of the boiler grate.

◆ Climb down the drain into the pipe.

◆ Go forward 10 times until you emerge from the pipe.

◆ Look down, then hop from the pipe onto the rocks below.

◆ Turn left and follow the path to a balcony.

◆ Climb over the railing, turn around, and click twice on the floor hatch for a close-up. Click on its handle to open it. This provides access to the beach via a tall ladder.

◆ Climb down the ladder to the beach.

- Follow the beach around to the pier.

- Return to the central valve controls at the end of the pier.

- Move the control handle to the rightmost position. This sends power to a device just off the balcony.

- Go back to the balcony ladder and climb up through the hatch.

- Open the double doors.

- Follow the walkway to the odd device—a frog trap.

gehn's frog trap

I've often wondered if frogs are smokable. I mean, what else could they be for? By the way, you needn't use this device to successfully complete Riven. But being an explorer driven by relentless curiosity, you can't resist the temptation to give it a try, can you? And it's such an amusing little device.

Here's how it works:

◆ Click on the top of the sphere to open the trap.

◆ Drag a food pellet from the container at right to the disk in the middle.

◆ Click on the handle at left to lower the trap.

◆ Wait a minute or two until you hear the trap spring.

◆ Click on the handle at left to raise the trap.

◆ If the trap is still open, click on the lever to lower it again. If the trap is shut, click on the top to open it and see the frog. Listen to the little fellow. Sound familiar?

Note the rattling fan above you. Annoying, isn't it? Let's shut off the darn thing. Not only will it be quieter, but the air shaft behind the fan will lead us to an interesting location.

◆ Go back up the walkway to the open double doors that lead out to the balcony.

◆ From inside, close the double doors. This reveals two hidden passages, one on either side.

◆ Enter the passage on the right. It leads outside to a walkway.

fan controls

◆ Move forward five times down the walkway to the lever on the right side. (You can vaguely hear the fan rattling.)

◆ Click on the lever to move it left. This turns off the fan.

Before we return to the fan duct, let's be ruthlessly efficient. First, we'll connect Book Assembly Island to the Golden Dome back on Temple Island. Then we'll cross and access the Temple Island Fire-marble Dome. Finally, we'll return to Book Assembly Island and examine the Fire-marble Dome there. Don't worry, the now-accessible fan duct will wait for you.

connect Book Assembly Island to Golden Dome

◆ Turn left from the fan control lever and follow the catwalk past Gehn's locked laboratory (at right), then through the tunnel.

◆ Cross the long footbridge to the raised drawbridge at the Golden Dome.

◆ Click on the handle at right to lower the bridge. (You directed power to this bridge back in Chapter 1, "Temple Island.")

◆ Cross the bridge to the Golden Dome.

◆ Unfortunately, you must swap disks here. Disk-swapping is a small price to pay for nonlinear worlds of fun. Put in Disc 2 and continue.

◆ Follow the walkway around the curve to its end.

◆ Turn the wheel to extend the walkway.

◆ Cross this newly extended walkway and take the first left. This is the doorway where you first entered the Golden Dome from the Gate Room back in Chapter 1.

◆ Push up the lever at right. This raises the bridge between the Golden Dome and the Gate Room to a new position for later.

◆ Turn around and go back to the main walkway.

◆ Turn right and go forward five times to the first right turn.

◆ Turn right and go to the gap in the walkway just outside the dome.

◆ Turn around and press the button at right. The missing section of the walkway rises into place.

◆ Continue down the walkway to the closed door.

◆ Throw the switch to open the door.

◆ Turn around and follow the walkway back into the Golden Dome. At the intersection, turn left and follow the walkway down stairs and out the lower level door.

◆ Continue along the walkway to the tunnel opening.

◆ Turn right and press the wall button to lower yourself to another, lower tunnel entry.

◆ Proceed through the lower tunnel and climb the metal stairs to the Fire-marble Dome.

fire-marble Dome (Temple island)

◆ Click on the kinetoscope to see the yellow-highlighted symbol— a circle with a dot in the center. Note the symbol well.

◆ Go back into the tunnel and push the button to raise yourself back to the upper level.

◆ Retrace your route around the inside of the Golden Dome to the long bridge that leads back to Book Assembly. (Here you must swap back to *Riven* Disc 1.)

◆ Cross the bridge to Book Assembly Island.

fire-marble Dome (Book Assembly island)

◆ Retrace your steps along the walkway past Gehn's laboratory (now on your left) back to the closed double doors.

◆ Go straight ahead into the other secret passage and follow it down to the Fire-marble Dome. Hmmm. Where's the kinetoscope?

If you follow the walkway to the left of the spinning dome, you can see the lens of the kinetoscope in the rock wall. But how do we get to it? Look up at the ceiling and note the shape of the crater opening. This is a helpful clue for a later puzzle.

◆ Return to the door and close it. Aha! Another secret passage leading right.

◆ Enter the passage and follow the tunnel to the kinetoscope.

◆ As before, click on the viewer for a close-up; then click on the top button when the yellow-highlighted symbol appears. This stops all the spinning.

◆ Again, note the highlighted symbol for later. Here, it's a circle with a vertical line.

◆ Exit the room and go back to Gehn's frog trap.

gehn's frog trap: fan passage

◆ Look up at the fan. It should be off now.

◆ Click on the fan duct to enter.

◆ Follow the duct to the next grate.

◆ Click on the grate to open it.

◆ Go through the grate into the laboratory.

gehn's laboratory

Gehn's lab contains a wealth of information. Examine and read everything. From his writings you can tell that Gehn's no raving lunatic, but he's definitely got a major god complex.

◆ Approach the desk and note the wooden eye.

◆ Click on the eye and note the symbol on the back. By now, you know it's the D'ni numeral 1. But what creature does it correspond to?

◆ Click on the paper under the eye.

◆ Read the paper.

Aha! Gehn found this eye by looking through the scope in his Survey Room. If you were observant back at Village Lake, you probably noticed a periscope-like thing protruding from the lake's center. Could that be Gehn's survey scope? If so, maybe we can use it to see where the replacement wooden eye is located and learn the missing creature in our five-creature sequence.

◆ Click on Gehn's laboratory journal to open it.

◆ Read the journal. Learn more about the Star Fissure, the D'ni preoccupation with five, Gehn's "233rd world" (the haven where he's built his new office), the Black Moiety rebellion, and other topics.

◆ *Important:* In the journal, note the "coded access system" of five D'ni numbers.

◆ Translate these five D'ni numbers into your numbers. (See the "Village Schoolroom" section of Chapter 2, "Jungle Island," for a translation of D'ni numerals.)

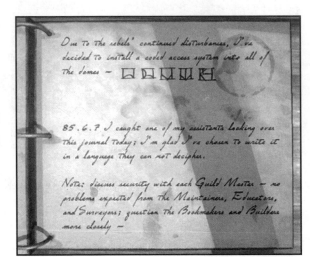

This code changes with each game of Riven

This five-number sequence is the code that opens the Fire-marble Domes. Remember those linking books you've glimpsed within the domes? In each dome, an inner seal slides into place with a slider lock. You must position the five sliders according to this five-digit combination to unlock the dome. Note, however, that this number sequence changes each time you play a new game of *Riven*, so I can't give you the exact code. Be sure to write down the sequence *in order*. Remember, you can't take the journal with you.

◆ Click on the front door (behind the tram call orb) to unlock it.

◆ Click on the blue button atop the orb to call the tram.

◆ Exit through the door across the room and proceed down the
  stairs to the waiting tram.

◆ Click on the knob to turn the tram car 180 degrees.

◆ Push the lever to ride the tram to Survey Island.

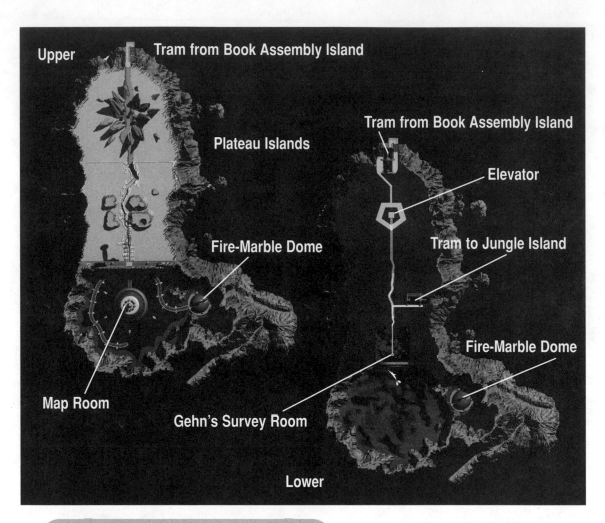

Upper

Tram from Book Assembly Island

Plateau Islands

Tram from Book Assembly Island

Elevator

Fire-Marble Dome

Tram to Jungle Island

Fire-Marble Dome

Map Room

Gehn's Survey Room

Lower

chapter four

survey island

This is my favorite island of all time. I like it better than St. Croix, frankly. The wild morphing map devices and oceanfront views are priceless and exhilarating. Figuring out what the maps *mean* is another matter, however. You won't find a more insidious set of visual puzzles in all of computer gaming. Fortunately, neither you nor I suffer from the kind of pride that keeps one from, say, *cheating*. So read on.

Arrival

◆ Exit the tram and follow the passage up the steps.

◆ Continue along the path through the spectacular rock formation.

◆ Move down the trench-like path to the huge building. Note the stone plateaus that rise from the lake on either side of the path.

◆ Enter the elevator and click on the button at lower left to ride up.

Map viewing Balcony

◆ Exit the elevator.

◆ Go to the edge of the balcony.

◆ Aha. Those plateaus you saw are actually maps of Riven's five islands. But the coolness is just beginning. Check out that control panel with five buttons, one for each island. Get ready for *weird physics!*

◆ Press a button and watch what happens. Weird water on the corresponding plateau island morphs up into a 3-D topographical map.

◆ Now turn around and proceed through the elevator to the far side. You'll find another lake, this one with a rust-colored building in the center.

◆ Continue down the walkway into the building.

map chamber

◆ Enter the chamber and approach the control panel. Note that the map shown on the panel corresponds to the plateau island you just extruded to three dimensions outside.

◆ Press any square to see a 3-D map of that square shoot up.

◆ Use the handle to view the selected 3-D map from different angles.

◆ Note also that each 3-D square is further divided into a 5-by-5 grid.

What does all this mean? Your task here is to note the exact grid location of the Fire-marble Dome on each of the five island maps. You need this information to solve a later puzzle. (Of course, you haven't actually *reached* the fifth island, yet. But it's so tiny, your educated guess at the Fire-marble Dome location should be pretty close to correct.) If you've paid close attention to the topography around each Fire-marble Dome during your exploration, this shouldn't be too difficult.

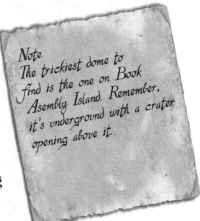

Note
The trickiest dome to find is the one on Book Asembly Island. Remember, it's underground with a crater opening above it.

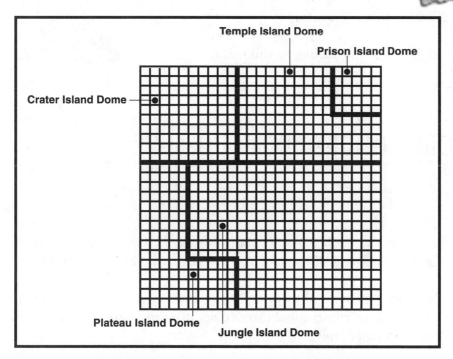

- ◆ Exit the Map Chamber and go to the walkway intersection.

- ◆ Turn right and continue to the Fire-marble Dome.

fire-marble dome (survey island)

◆ Examine the dome. Note the highlighted symbol—a circle with a horizontal line—for later.

◆ Turn around and follow the walkway around the lake to the kinetoscope. Unfortunately, this one is broken.

◆ Return to the elevator.

◆ Ride down and return to the tram.

Tram stations/secret passage

◆ Enter the tram.

◆ Click on the knob to rotate the tram car 180 degrees. Don't push the handle forward, though! You aren't leaving Plateau Island yet.

◆ Turn left and exit the tram. That's right, you're now on ... *the other side of the tracks!* (You've spent your entire life trying to find this place, haven't you?)

◆ Go through the door and take two steps down the corridor to the striped lever at left.

◆ Pull the lever to raise a gleaming, golden elevator car. Damn, it's beautiful.

◆ Enter the elevator and push the button to activate the car.

◆ When the elevator stops, exit and follow the long passage.

◆ Watch for a startled man.

This hooded fellow is one of Gehn's many minions. Follow him down the side passage if you want; you can't catch him, but he leads you to another tram station, where he escapes in a tram car. Note the location. This tram line runs back to Jungle Island, and you'll use it shortly.

◆ Return to the main passage and turn left.

◆ Follow the passage up the stairs to the underwater room.

gehn's survey room

◆ Click on the chair to sit in it.

◆ Push the red button at the right to rotate and raise the chair.

◆ Click on the knob-topped lever at the right to lower a color wheel.

◆ Look down for a close-up of the color wheel.

Do any of the symbols on the wheel look familiar? Yes, you've seen some of them on the Fire-marble Domes you've discovered on various Riven islands.

◆   Click on the tab just outside any symbol. The color wheel turns, moving that symbol to the active position—that is, to the bottom.

◆   Click on the active symbol to illuminate the colored underwater lamp associated with it.

◆   Repeat this process with each symbol. Note the color associated with each symbol. Note also that one lamp is out of order.

Obviously, each Fire-marble Dome is associated with a particular color. Below is a list of symbol/color associations:

SYMBOL	COLOR	DOME ON ISLAND
	Blue	Prison
	Green	Temple
	Yellow	None
	Orange	Survey
	Red	Jungle
	(Broken)	Book Assembly

Note that when you click on red, a hungry wahrk appears. For fun, do it at least four times. (After that, the big slug wises up and won't return for awhile.)

◆ Click on the right lever again to raise the wheel.

◆ Click on the left lever to lower a viewer.

◆ Look down and click on the left button to see Catherine, wife of Atrus, in her prison chamber. At last! (Careful: *Myst* fans may burst into tears here.)

◆ Click on the right-hand button to view Jungle Island from Village Lake.

◆ Click on the tabs to rotate the view until you see the outline of a fish (created by a cave and its watery reflection).

Aha! Fish! The missing creature symbol! And that tiny white object near the left tip is the fifth wooden eye; you can't reach the eye, but you don't need to. You've already seen the eye's number in Gehn's lab. You know it's 1.

◆ Click on the left lever again to raise the viewer.

◆ Push the red button at right to lower the chair.

◆ Go forward to exit the chair.

◆ Descend the stairs and return to the tram station where Gehn's hooded minion escaped—for the memory-impaired, that's the first doorway on the right side of the passage.

◆ Press the blue button on the tram call.

◆ Board the tram car when it arrives.

◆ Rotate the tram 180 degrees and ride it to Jungle Island.

chapter five

The Moiety Age

Arrival at Jungle Island

The first thing you do is swap to *Riven* Disc 3. Then start your rebel hunt.

◆ Exit the tram and go through the door to the elevator.

◆ Ride up one level. You end up inside the wahrk idol.

◆ Exit the idol and follow the path through the forest (turning right at the Y-intersection under the Fire-marble Dome) beyond the wooden gate.

◆ Turn right and follow the wooden walkway through the eerie, blue-lit cavern to the ladder.

◆ Climb up the ladder and return to the holding cell.

◆ Click on the floor of the cage to open the grate.

◆ Click on the water to pull the ring and open the secret door on the cage's back wall.

◆ Enter the tunnel and follow it to the stone pillar room.

stone pillar room (gate to moiety age)

Click on the stone pillars in the following order: fish, bug, frog, sunner, wahrk. The water drains from the far wall. Then a panel opens revealing a rock shelf with an open book.

◆ Click on the book to see the Moiety Age. (Yes, that's the awesome organic structure on the cover of the game box.)

◆ Click on the book again to proceed to the Moiety Age.

The Moiety Age

◆ Time for *Riven* Disc 5. Go ahead, swap. I'll wait for you right here.

◆ Turn around and enter the room with the idol.

◆ Approach the idol, then turn around to see Moiety rebels. *Zap!*

◆ Nothing like a dart in the neck to give you the rest you so sorely need. You briefly regain consciousness in a boat floating toward the big, tree-like structure. Go back to sleep. You're fully immersed in Riven politics now. Rest up.

◆ Go to the locked front door. Welcome to Pod World!

◆ Face the table in the middle of the room. A woman brings you Catherine's journal and the Prison Book you lost in the game's opening sequence.

◆ Read the journal.

Catherine's writings provide a wealth of back-story information. You learn all about the rebellion against Gehn, a movement the natives call the "Black Moiety." Note the important mention of a "small mechanical stop"—a locking pin—for the telescope back at the Star Fissure. Note also the sequence of five D'ni numerals, a combination for the locked viewport of the telescope. (This combination changes with each new game of Riven, so I can't give it to you here.) And finally, note that the combination to release Catherine is kept in Gehn's office.

This code changes with every Riven game.

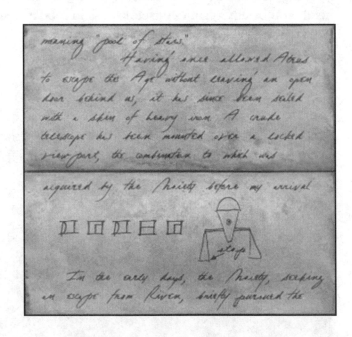

◆ Look up from the journal. The Black Moiety woman returns with a linking book to the stone pillar room on Jungle Island.

◆ Click twice on the picture to return to the stone pillar room.

Back to Jungle Island

OK, now you have almost everything you need for your showdown with Gehn—the Prison Book, the locations of the Fire-marble Domes on the grid map, two five-numeral sequences of D'ni numbers, and the colors associated with each island. Of course, if you were playing without help, you'd have to guess the Prison Island color. But who's insane enough to play a game like *Riven* without help?

Let's head back to Temple Island.

◆ Exit the pillar room and follow the tunnel to the secret door.

◆ Click on the ring to open the door. Then go through the prison cell.

◆ Turn right and follow the walkway to the ladder.

◆ Descend the ladder and turn around.

◆ Follow the walkway through the eerie, blue-lit cave.

◆ Continue past the wooden gate at left, up the stairs, and out of the forest.

◆ Cross the suspension bridge and go forward four times down the stone stairway.

◆ Turn left to the cave opening and enter.

◆ Just inside the cave opening, press the blue tram call button.

◆ Continue down the stairs to the tram station.

◆ Board the tram, turn it around, and ride to Temple Island.

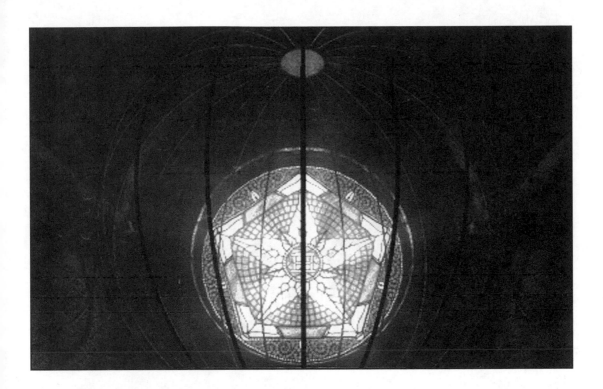

chapter six

Gehn's Age

Arrival at Temple Island

◆ Exit the tram from Jungle Island.

◆ Climb the stairs into the Temple. The door opens, revealing a man's face in the imager. Gehn! Man, that guy's everywhere.

◆ Inside the door, turn left and click on the door between the pillars. (It's directly under the leftmost lantern.)

◆ Follow the dank passage up the stairs, past the throne room door on the right.

◆ Continue across the bridge into the Gate Room.

The Gate Room

If you're following this walkthrough, the Gate Room's inner chamber should be set so you can enter the Gate Room and go through the correct doorway on the far side. If not, push the button to rotate the inner chamber so the far doorway lies to the left.

◆ Cross the Gate Room and go through the far doorway.

◆ Follow the raised ramp up to the narrow entry in the Golden Dome.

Note
In this walkthrough, you raised the ramp to this setting when you connected Book Assembly Island to the Golden Dome and adjusted the bridges. See "Book Assembly Island to Golden Dome" in Chapter 3, "Book Assembly."

◆ Move down the narrow corridor. Note the lever on the right-hand wall; don't use it yet.

◆ Approach the marble grid puzzle.

◆ Click on the puzzle for a close-up.

marble puzzle

Does this grid arrangement look familiar? You saw the same 25-by-25 array in the Map Chamber on Survey Island. To solve the marble puzzle, you must remember the exact grid locations of the five Fire-marble Domes from the Survey Island 3-D topographical maps; match five marbles by color to the five islands (based on the color wheel scheme in Gehn's Survey Room); then place the appropriate colored marbles in the corresponding Fire-marble Dome squares on the puzzle grid.

Sound complicated? It is.

But don't worry. Because you were kind enough to buy this book, I'll be happy to give you the answers.

Place the marbles according to the following diagram:

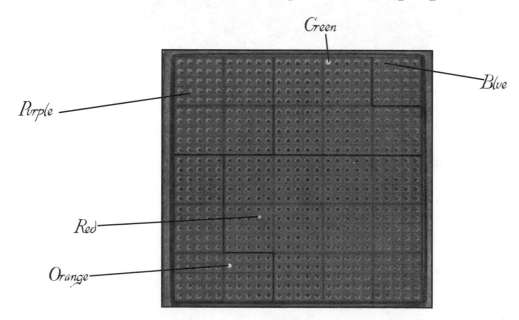

◆ Turn around and go to the wall switch in the corridor.

◆ Click on the wall switch to lower the marble press and reveal the white button.

◆ Click on the white button to activate the press.

A spectacular wind blast indicates you've placed the marbles correctly and have powered up all five Fire-marble Domes. Now you can use any of the linking books in the domes—as long as you have the code to *open* the domes, of course. Again, this code changes from game to game in *Riven*, so Cheat Boy can't help you there. The five-number code was in Gehn's journal in his laboratory on Book Assembly Island. If you haven't found the code yet, or you forgot to jot it down, then you'll have to go there now to get it.

Otherwise, your obvious next task is to return to any one of the four Fire-marble Domes you've previously visited in Riven. The quickest trip is probably to the dome right here on Temple Island.

◆ Turn around, exit the Golden Dome, and return down the ramp into the Gate Room.

◆ Exit through the far door and turn around to see the chamber rotation button.

◆ Push the button three times.

This rotates the chamber so one doorway is in front of you and the other doorway is on the back right wall of the Gate Room as you enter.

◆ Go through the far door of the Gate Room.

◆ Follow the catwalk into the Golden Dome. (You created this access back in the "Connect Book Assembly to Golden Dome" section of Chapter 3, "Book Assembly Island.")

◆ At the intersection, turn left and follow the curving catwalk around to the stairs.

◆ Descend the stairs and continue out of the dome.

◆ Follow the outside walkway to the tunnel entrance and turn right to face the lift button.

◆ Push the button to ride the lift down to the lower-level tunnel.

◆ Turn left, exit the tunnel, and climb the stairs to the Fire-marble Dome.

fire-marble Dome (Temple Island)

◆ Approach the slider puzzle on the dome.

◆ Move the sliders to the positions on the scale that match the five-number sequence you found in Gehn's lab journal on Book Assembly Island.

◆ Push the button under the sliders.

◆ Click on the linking book for a close-up. Watch the spectacular fly-by sequence of Gehn's world.

◆ Click on the animated window to travel to Gehn's age.

Gehn's Age: office

You arrive inside a cage, of course. Gehn's twisted, but he's not stupid. Note his linking books to each of the five islands of Riven arrayed around the cage. You can identify each by the grid pattern you first saw on the plaque in the Golden Dome, then in the map devices on Survey Island.

◆ After you arrive, turn left twice to the button.

◆ Push the button to summon Gehn.

◆ Listen to Gehn's sorry excuse for a story. When he asks you to use the Prison Book first, click on its animated window. (If you wait too long, Gehn closes the Prison Book, powers up all the other linking books, and exits to give you more time to think and/or explore. But that's OK. Just push the call button again; he'll be back.)

When Gehn attempts to follow you through the link, you switch places with him—he's trapped in the book, you're free in his office.

◆ Turn right and approach the big globe-like device.

◆ In the close-up, click on the lever, sliding it to the right. This powers up all the linking books.

◆ Turn right and move toward the window. See the switch handle?

◆ Pull the switch handle to lower the cage into the floor.

◆ Turn right and approach the well-like passage.

◆ Climb down the ladder to Gehn's bedroom.

gehn's bedroom

◆ Read Gehn's personal journal on the nightstand next to his bed.

◆ Click on the small metal globe next to the journal. Listen *carefully* to the sequence of five sounds; jot down a description. This is the code that unlocks Catherine's prison.

◆ Climb back up the ladder to the office.

◆ Find the linking book for Prison Island. It's the book with a single square as its grid pattern.

◆ Open the linking book and click on the animated window to travel to Prison Island.

chapter seven

prison island & star fissure finale
Arrival at prison island

This tiny island has split off far from the rest of the Riven chain. You
arrive inside the Fire-marble Dome.

◆ Press the floor button under the linking book podium. You rise out of the dome.

◆ Follow the walkway to the elevator.

◆ Enter the elevator to see a sound device with three keys, a small lever, and a bar attached to a pull-cord.

◆ Use the keys to enter the sequence of five sounds you heard when you opened the small globe-shaped watch on Gehn's nightstand.

◆ Click on the lever to open the cage. The elevator automatically travels up to Catherine's room.

Meet Catherine, wife of Atrus, goddess of the Moiety. She hustles onto the elevator, pulls the cord, and you ride back down together. And off she goes!

◆ Go back out to the Fire-marble Dome. Because Catherine just used it, it's spinning again.

◆ Use the kinetoscope as before; look in the viewer. When the high-lighted symbol appears, click on the top button to stop the spinning and retract the outer dome.

◆ Approach the dome and reset the slider puzzle to the same five-number sequence you used earlier.

◆ Open the linking book and use it to return to Gehn's age.

You arrive in the cage again, but don't freak out. Turn until you find the Temple Island linking book and click on it to get a close-up; it's the one with this grid pattern:

◆   Open the Temple Island linking book.

◆   Click on the animated window to travel to Temple Island.

Temple Island

◆   Click on the floor button to exit the Fire-marble Dome.

◆   Turn around and follow the walkway to the wall button.

◆ Press the wall button to lower the lift.

◆ Step forward onto the lift and press the button again to go up one level.

◆ Turn right and follow the walkway into the Golden Dome.

◆ Follow the catwalk around the inside of the dome to the raised drawbridge.

◆ Pull the lever to lower the drawbridge and cross it into the Gate Room.

◆ Exit the Gate Room through the far door and turn right.

◆ Go down the stairs to the Star Fissure platform (where you started the game).

star fissure platform

◆ Approach the telescope.

◆ Click on the floor hatch for a close-up.

◆ Think of the buttons as being numbered 1 to 5, from left to right.

◆ Use the telescope code from Catherine's journal to click the buttons in the correct order based on the numbering you did in the previous step.

◆ Click on the handle to open the hatch.

◆ Move back from the hatch and click on the viewfinder to see the star field in the fissure. Cool! (Remember the opening sequence of *Myst*?)

◆ Move back again.

◆ Click on the strut just left of the hatch for a close-up. What's that thing stuck in there? That wouldn't be a *locking pin*, would it?

◆ Click on the handle to retract the locking pin.

◆ Move back again.

◆ Click on the control lever at far right.

◆ Click on the control button (just below the lever) five times to lower the telescope through the glass and start the sundering.

Thus ends your *Riven* adventure. Unlike *Myst*, *Riven* wraps with a comforting sense of closure. Gehn is banished. Catherine and Atrus are back together. Her people are safe. He is visibly relieved and grateful.

Your work is done. And so is mine.

one-on-one with cyan

Q Many critics/fans have likened *Myst* to *The Hobbit*, pointing to *Riven* as a Tolkien-like expansion of your universe. Is a *Lord of the Rings* type universe something you'd like to emulate?

A Rand Miller: Only to the extent that we want to build very complete worlds. *Lord of the Rings* is so satisfying because of the detail. You get the feeling that the world you're reading about is real. Different but real. That's how we go about designing. It's not just a game for us, it's an entire world wrapped around the part that becomes the actual product.

Q Do you feel artistically satisfied with *Myst* and *Riven*—that is, are they fundamental expressions of your creative energies? If you had unlimited resources, what would you set as your next challenge?

A Robyn Miller: I believe we achieved our goals almost as much as is possible. But I don't believe it's possible to be 100 percent there when you're dealing with budgets and schedules (which are both extremely necessary on a project with more than one person working on it). If we made 80 percent or 90 percent, then I'm thrilled. We achieved more on this project than we've ever achieved before, and even it if it fails in the market, I will have felt like we were successful.

Q What inspires you to create?

A Rand Miller: The same thing that inspires everyone to create. That moment when you've just poured everything you've got into finishing something, and you take a step back and can say that it's good. It's a feeling of Biblical proportions. Of course, then you rest!

Q Are there any specific books, movies, artists, or musicians who particularly inspire you?

A Rand Miller: Myst was inspired only remotely by *Mysterious Island*, in that Robyn had read the book shortly before our design work started. *Riven* was inspired by many things, mostly subconscious, but it was much more of a purposeful work. What I mean by that is, the creative effort entailed a much larger degree of asking ourselves "why." So that before creating a building, or animal, or tool, we wanted to know who built it, why it was built, what materials would it likely be made of, etc.

Q Can you name other specific sources of inspiration for the *Myst/Riven* universe you've created?

A Robyn Miller: We have stacks and stacks of books in our art department, and we rely on them heavily during both the design and production phases of our work. We most heavily referenced books relating to African, Arabic, and Celtic designs. But I can't say we didn't spend a good deal of time looking through books on the making of *Star Wars*. Seriously, these *Star Wars* books offer us a lot of indirect inspiration because the films (or, at least, a couple of them) were designed in such a visually superior fashion.

Q The images in both *Myst* and *Riven* are gorgeous, but more importantly, the pictures themselves tell a story—a story with remarkable depth. One could argue that topography and architecture actually tell the bulk of the story in *Riven*. Is your focus on such visual storytelling by design?

A Richard Vander Wende: Yes, one of the inherent strengths of this type of non-linear experience is that the participant's relationship with the environment can be much more intimate than it can with traditional linear media. One of our conscious goals with *Riven* was to imbue the environment with as much story as we could: we were curious as to what the possible cumulative effects of this would be. Would it be possible to communicate enough material that the participant might conceivably begin to feel emotions? It was an intriguing idea, and we only scratched the surface of it.

Q *Myst* attracted a huge audience of first-time gamers. Did you have this audience of non-gamers in mind when you designed *Riven*?

A Rand Miller: A grandmother in Montana, here in the U.S., wrote to say she could not stop playing *Myst*. (She never played computer games before.) She actually had neglected her household duties for a week because she was so enamored with the adventure. I don't think that we consciously designed *Riven* around these first-time gamers, but we certainly wanted to make *Riven* as playable as *Myst* was.

Q Do you play many computer games? If so, do you have any favorite games?

A Richard Vander Wende: Not really. Robyn and I are not really into games of any kind. We're more interested in building worlds. To us, *Myst* and now *Riven* are not 'games' at all, we certainly didn't think of them as such as we were working on *Riven*. They're more like virtual theme parks or something ... I wish there was a better term for these things because I think the word 'game' is kind of misleading, especially to those non-gamers who are looking at these things from the outside, trying to figure out if it's something that they might enjoy or not.

Q What does the future hold for Cyan? Will you continue to focus on software and games?

A Rand Miller: We're all ready for a vacation—we haven't thought about what is next. It feels like we just gave birth (if I can be so presumptuous as to assume how much pain that is) and now we're ready to sit back and enjoy the baby for a while.

Q Will there be another sequel?

A Robyn Miller: We do not plan on doing one at all. The story ends with *Riven*. If we keep creating in that place, it may end up being forced and just plain bad. I've been immersed in the *Myst/Riven* universe for seven years now. It's time to move on and get to something fresh and new. We get excited with the idea of starting with a blank sheet.

Q Marketing types would call the *Myst/Riven* universe you've created a 'property.' Do you have any George Lucas-like aspirations to expand it into another media? If you could create a universe totally different from *Myst's*, what would it be like?

A Rand Miller: Can't tell you because that's what we'll be working on next! (Ha, ha!)

Q Here's your chance to slam all of us parasites who've ridden on the *Myst* gravy train the past few years. If you could write an authoritative strategy guide to *Riven* (or *Myst*), how would you approach it? What would you include?

A Rand Miller: Any kind of guide to *Riven* or *Myst* would be based on one person's experience. That's what I would want to follow. It would give me insight into what someone else did that might help me with my journey. But it's just what they did, what they thought, what they saw, it doesn't imply that it's the right way, just one person's journey through the world. But of course the best way is to avoid using the guide at all. Just take your time and enjoy the journey. (I can say that now that you've already bought the guide, right?)

To Order Books

Please send me the following items:

Quantity	Title	Unit Price	Total
_____	_____	$ _____	$ _____
_____	_____	$ _____	$ _____
_____	_____	$ _____	$ _____
_____	_____	$ _____	$ _____
_____	_____	$ _____	$ _____

Subtotal	$ _____
Deduct 10% when ordering 3-5 books	$ _____
7.25% Sales Tax (CA only)	$ _____
8.25% Sales Tax (TN only)	$ _____
5.0% Sales Tax (MD and IN only)	$ _____
7.0% G.S.T. Tax (Canada only)	$ _____
Shipping and Handling*	$ _____
Total Order	$ _____

*Shipping and Handling depend on Subtotal.

Subtotal	Shipping/Handling
$0.00–$14.99	$3.00
$15.00–$29.99	$4.00
$30.00–$49.99	$6.00
$50.00–$99.99	$10.00
$100.00–$199.99	$13.50
$200.00+	Call for Quote

Foreign and all Priority Request orders:
Call Order Entry department
for price quote at 916-632-4400

This chart represents the total retail price of books only
(before applicable discounts are taken).

By Telephone: With MC or Visa, call 800-632-8676 or 916-632-4400. Mon–Fri, 8:30-4:30.
WWW: http://www.primapublishing.com

By Internet E-mail: sales@primapub.com
By Mail: Just fill out the information below and send with your remittance to:

Prima Publishing
P.O. Box 1260BK
Rocklin, CA 95677

My name is _____

I live at _____

City _____ State _____ ZIP _____

MC/Visa# _____ Exp. _____

Check/money order enclosed for $ _____ Payable to Prima Publishing

Daytime telephone _____

Signature _____